AT THE CAFÉ:
CONVERSATIONS
ON ANARCHISM
BY ERRICO MALATESTA

FREEDOM PRESS

AT THE CAFÉ: CONVERSATIONS ON ANARCHISM BY ERRICO MALATESTA

Edited with an introduction

by Paul Nursey-Bray

Translated by Paul Nursey-Bray
with the assistance of Piero Ammirato

Graphic Design and Photographs by Nilla Westin
Published 2005 by Freedom Press
84B Whitechapel High Street, London E1 7QX

ISBN 1 904491 06 5

Printed in Great Britain by Aldgate Press
Units 5/6 Gunthorpe Workshops, Gunthorpe Street, London E1 7RQ

CONTENTS

INTRODUCTION

Malatesta began writing the series of dialogues that make up *At the Café: Conversations on Anarchism* in March 1897, while he was in hiding in Ancona and busy with the production of the periodical *L'Agitazione*. Luigi Fabbri, in his account of this period, written to introduce the 1922 edition of the full set of dialogues (*Bologna, Edizioni di Volontà*), edited by Malatesta (*Reprint, Torino, Sargraf, 1961*), gives us a beguiling picture of Malatesta, clean-shaven as a disguise, coming and going about the city, pipe in mouth, smiling impudently at his friends, who, for the sake of his safety, wished him elsewhere.

The idea of the dialogues was suggested to him by the fact that he often frequented a café that was not usually the haunt of subversives such as himself. Indeed, one of the regulars, who was a member of the police, used to engage Malatesta in conversation without, of course, as Fabbri notes, any idea that a real prize lay within his grasp. Anarchism would almost certainly been one of the topics of conversation since the anarchists of the city constantly bombarded their fellow townspeople with a barrage of propaganda that occasioned frequent trials.

The form that the dialogues were to take was drawn then from an actual venue and from Malatesta's own experience. It resulted in a literary device excellently well suited to his particular genius, which is his ability to render complex ideas into straightforward language and to make them directly accessible. The dialogue form also allowed Malatesta to debate the ideas of his opponents, while subjecting his own anarchist views to a critical scrutiny aimed at communicating to his readers their political import and their practical applicability. Indeed one of the strengths of the dialogues is the absence of straw men. The inquisition of anarchism is searching and genuine, often highlighting what its opponents would regard as points of weakness and vulnerability. It makes Malatesta's spirited defence all the more impressive.

Towards the end of 1897 Malatesta was identified and discovered by the Ancona police. He was arrested and then released. Immediately he began a round of lectures, abandoning both his journal and the unfinished dialogues. In 1898 he was placed under house arrest and in March 1899 he fled abroad, once more becoming a refugee. The dialogues remained interrupted at number ten, and in this form they were published, both in journals and as a pamphlet.

The chief propagandists of the first ten dialogues are Malatesta's alter ego, Giorgio, an anarchist, Prospero, a wealthy member of the bourgeoisie, Cesare, a shopkeeper and Ambrogio, a magistrate. Malatesta is thus able to reflect a range of political positions and views drawn from a wide spectrum of society. If Prospero speaks for wealth and privilege, Cesare speaks for the smaller property owners and the middle classes. He shows an awareness of social problems and appears amenable to persuasion by Giorgio, but he also exhibits a concern that any solution must not be allowed to disrupt the existing social order. Ambrogio is the voice of the law and the liberal state and of accepted ideas on rights and justice. He is also, as Giorgio's chief opponent, the one who expresses common sense views about human nature and human behaviour. His views contain a liberal expression of rights theory, tempered by what he would claim as recognition of the limits imposed on liberty by the inescapable dictates of reality. The result is a broad canvas on which Malatesta is able, in responding to the various viewpoints and in answering the numerous criticisms that Giorgio's views elicit, to paint a skilfully drawn and detailed picture of an anarchist view of the world.

In a relatively short space Malatesta introduces us to all of the basic doctrines of communist anarchism and considers one by one many of the major objections to his position. After setting the scene, it is private property and property rights that become the focus of attention. In Dialogues Two, Three and Four it is argued that the causes of poverty are located in the nature of the property system and its associated class structure and a forceful attack is mounted on the right to private property and the capitalist system, with incidental discussions of Malthus and free trade. At the same time the notions of a complete change in the property regime and the creation of a society without government are introduced. The origin of property and property rights are considered in Dialogue Five, and Giorgio maintains that property rights must be abolished if exploitation is to be avoided. In Dialogue Six the case for common ownership is made and the idea of communism introduced. This discussion of communism continues in Dialogue Seven with opposition to it as a tyrannical and oppressive system being strongly maintained by Ambrogio in the name of abstract liberty. Giorgio counters with a depiction of anarchist society as a voluntary, complex federation of associations, and in the process contrasts the anarchist form of free communism with that of the authoritarian school. Dialogue Eight moves the focus to the question of government and the state and how a society can function in their absence. In the process there is an extended critique of parliamentarianism and representation, and a defence of anarchism as a social order maintained by free agreement and voluntary delegation. The argument continues into the next Dialogue (Dialogue Nine) where the objections to a society without government are again rehearsed and Giorgio further develops a form of Kropotkin's argument about the universality of mutual aid, an idea first introduced in Dialogue Six. Discourse Ten strikes out in a new direction, focussing on sex, love and the family. In covering many issues related to feminism any inherent basis for gender inequality is persuasively dismissed.

It was 15 years later, in 1913, that Malatesta returned to the dialogues. At this time he had once more established himself in Ancona and had begun the publication of his new journal *Volontà*. In this new publication he republished the original ten dialogues, in an edited and corrected form, and added four more. Initially, in Dialogues Eleven and Twelve, it is once again Cesare, Prospero and Ambrogio who are Giorgio's interlocutors. The issue of criminality is raised in Dialogue Eleven. How do we deal with criminals in the absence of government, law, courts or prisons? Giorgio answers that the issue must be dealt with communally. From here the discussion moves on to a contrast between mental and manual labour and the old chestnut of who is to do the jobs that nobody wants to do. Won't everyone want to be a poet? The usual answer is provided, that is a voluntary rotation of tasks and the development of multiple skills by community members. Dialogue Twelve investigates the need for revolution, and a case is made for the sad necessity of a violent revolution, since the existing order is maintained by violence and the privileged classes will not surrender their hold on power unless it is shaken loose.

In Dialogue Thirteen we meet a new character, Vincenzo, a young Republican, and a discussion ensues regarding the merits and limitations of a republican approach to change. Its chief defect is identified as a reliance on government and on systems of democratic representation. Republicanism is not, it is argued, as radical as its supporters believe since it remains prey to the evils of the existing political system. The last dialogue of this new series (Dialogue Fourteen) returns to the theme of revolution. What Giorgio emphasises is that anarchism in its desire to remove the state and government is a new factor in history and proposes changes quite different and more profound than previous revolutions which aimed simply at changing the political regime.

Once more the dialogues were to be interrupted by political events. In June 1914, as the storm clouds of World War I gathered, serious popular risings broke out in the Marches and Romagna, in what became known as Red Week. Malatesta was involved in these popular struggles and, as a result, was forced to take refuge in London. Six years passed and Malatesta returned to Italy, establishing himself in Milan, where he edited the Newspaper *Umanità Nova*. He was too busy, Fabbri notes, to give his attention to the old dialogues, and he did not intend to add to them. However, Fabbri informs us that someone or other who spent a fortnight with him as a guest persuaded him to continue with the project. The mysterious guest must, one would think, have been Fabbri himself. The result was a further three dialogues, a continuation rather than a conclusion, since there is no obvious point of closure.

In these last three essays some old topics are revisited and some new themes, of contemporary significance, receive attention. Dialogue Fifteen introduces Gino, a worker, and canvasses the fears of ordinary people about a lack of civil order in the proposed stateless society and the perceived need for police. Police, Malatesta argues through Giorgio, breed criminals, just as he had argued earlier in *Anarchy* that the *louvreterie* (wolf catchers) breed wolves, since without wolves or criminals the survival of the respective bodies of officials would be in jeopardy (London, 1974: 33–34). Social defence, he asserts, is a community responsibility. The fact that this issue was already discussed in Dialogue Eleven is an indication of its importance to Malatesta. In Dialogue Sixteen we meet Pippo, a crippled war veteran, who opens up the questions of nationalism and patriotism. The points Malatesta makes here echo Lenin's call for class solidarity in the face of the divisive and destructive nationalism of the First World War. Giorgio makes it clear that in his view patriotism is simply a device by which the bourgeoisie recruits working class support for the existing property regime, and the territorial ambitions of those who benefit from it. Finally, in Dialogue Seventeen, Luigi, a socialist, enters and a discussion ensues that aims at distinguishing anarchism from both parliamentary and authoritarian socialism, but with the key focus on the inevitable failure of the parliamentary path and of any form of what Eduard Bernstein had called evolutionary socialism. The need for a revolutionary change is underlined.

Work on the dialogues in their present form was completed by October 1920. On 16 October Malatesta was arrested and placed in the prison of San Vittore. There was an extensive police search of his apartments for arms and explosives, but the manuscript of the dialogues remained undiscovered or ignored. They were published as a set, with Fabbri's introduction, in 1922.

These dialogues of Malatesta represent not just a major contribution to anarchist political theory, but a significant historical document. Written over a period of 23 years they are a commentary on turbulent times and vital historical events, covering as they do an epoch distinguished in particular by left-wing agitation and organisation across Europe. During the time spanned by these ruminations on anarchism the world witnessed the Second International, the rise of Bolshevism, the First World War, the birth of Fascism and the Russian Revolutions, both of 1904 and 1917. Without any direct allusion to any of these events the dialogues engage in a lively debate with many of the issues that they raise. In a real sense Malatesta has crafted anarchist theory into a running commentary on his times. It is a work of intelligence, style and real artistry.

Paul Nursey-Bray

ONE

PROSPERO [*A plump member of the bourgeoisie, full of political economy and other sciences*]: But of course... of course... we know all about it. There are people suffering from hunger, women prostituting themselves, children dying from a lack of care. You always say the same thing... in the end you become boring. Allow me to savour my gelati in peace... Certainly, there are a thousand evils in our society, hunger, ignorance, war, crime, plague, terrible mishaps ... so what? Why is it your concern?

MICHELE [*A student who keeps company with socialists and anarchists*]: I beg your pardon? Why is it my concern? You have a comfortable home, a well-provisioned table, servants at your command; for you everything is fine. And as long as you and yours are all right, even if the world around you collapses, nothing matters. Really, if you only had a little heart...

PROSPERO: Enough, enough... don't sermonise... Stop raging, young man. You think I am insensible, indifferent to the misfortunes of others. On the contrary, my heart bleeds, (waiter, bring me a cognac and a cigar), my heart bleeds; but the great social problems are not resolved by sentiment.

The laws of nature are immutable and neither great speeches, nor mawkish sentimentality can do anything about it. The wise person accepts fate, and gets the best out of life that he can, without running after pointless dreams.

MICHELE: Ah? So we are dealing with natural laws?... And what if the poor got it into their heads to correct these... laws of nature. I have heard speeches hardly supportive of these superior laws.

PROSPERO: Of course, of course. We well know the people with whom you associate. On my behalf, tell those scoundrel socialists and anarchists, who you have chosen to be your preferred company, that for them, and for those who would try to put in practice their wicked theories, we have good soldiers and excellent *carabinieri*.

MICHELE: Oh! If you are going to bring in the soldiers and the *carabinieri*, I won't talk anymore. It is like proposing a fist fight to demonstrate my opinions are in error. However, don't rely on brute force if you have no other arguments. Tomorrow you may find yourself in the weakest position; what then?

PROSPERO: What then? Well, if that misfortune should come about, there would be great disorder, an explosion of evil passions, massacres, looting... and then it would all return to how it was before. Maybe a few poor people would have become enriched, some rich people would have fallen into poverty, but overall nothing would have changed, because the world cannot change. Bring me, just bring me one of these anarchist agitators of yours and you will see how I will tan his hide. They are good at filling the heads of people like you with tall stories because your heads are empty; but you'll see whether they will be able to maintain their absurdities with me.

MICHELE: All right. I will bring a friend of mine who holds socialist and anarchist principles and I will promote your discussion with him with pleasure. In the meantime discuss matters with me, for while I still don't have well developed opinions, I clearly see that society as it is organized today, is a thing contrary to good sense and decency. Come now, you are so fat and flourishing that a bit of excitement will not do you any harm. It will help your digestion.

PROSPERO: Come on, then; let's have a discussion. But, you ought to know that it would be better if you studied instead of spitting out opinions about matters that are the province of others more learned and wiser. I believe I can give you 20 years?

MICHELE: This does not prove that you have studied more, and if I have to judge you from what you have been saying, I doubt that, even if you have studied a lot, you have gained much from it.

PROSPERO: Young man, young man, really! Let's have some respect.

MICHELE: All right, I respect you. But don't throw my age in my face, as if in fact you were raising an objection to me with the police. Arguments are not old or young, they are good or bad; that's all.

PROSPERO: Well, well, let's get on with what you have to say?

MICHELE: I must say that I cannot understand why the peasants that hoe, sow and harvest have neither sufficient bread, nor wine or meat; why bricklayers that build houses don't have a roof for shelter, why shoemakers have worn shoes. In other words, why is it that those who work, that produce everything, lack basic necessities; while those who don't do anything revel in abundance. I cannot understand why there are people that lack bread, when there is much uncultivated land and a lot of people who would be extremely happy to be able to cultivate it; why are there so many bricklayers out of work while there are lots of people who need houses; why many shoemakers, dressmakers etc... are without work, while the majority of the population lacks shoes, clothes and all the necessities of civil life. Could you please tell me which is the natural law that explains and justifies these absurdities?

PROSPERO: Nothing could be more clear and simple.

To produce, human labour is not enough, you need land, materials, tools, premises, machinery and you also need the means to survive while waiting for the product to be made and delivered to the market: in a word, you need capital. Your peasants, your workers, have only their physical labour; as a consequence they cannot work if such is not the wish of those who own land and capital. And since we are few in number and have enough even if, for a while, we leave our land uncultivated and our capital inoperative, while the workers are many and are always constrained by immediate needs, it follows that they must work whenever and however we wish and on whatever terms that suit us. And when we no longer need their labour and calculate that there is no gain from making them work, they are forced to remain idle even when they have the greatest need for the very things they could produce.

Are you content now? Could I explain it more clearly that this?

MICHELE: Certainly, this is what one calls speaking frankly, there is no question about that.

But, by what right does land belong only to a few? How is it that capital is found in a few hands, specifically in the hands of those who do not work?

PROSPERO: Yes, yes, I know what you are saying to me, and I even know the more or less lame arguments with which others would oppose you; the right of the owners derives from the improvement they bring to the land, from savings by means of which labour is transformed into capital, etc. But let me be even more frank. Things are as they are as the result of historical facts, the product of hundreds of years of human history. The whole of human existence has been, is, and will always be, a continuous struggle. There are those who have fared well and those who have fared badly. What can I do about it? So much the worse for some, so much the better for others. Woe to the conquered! This is the grand law of nature against which no revolt is possible.

What would you like? Should I deprive myself of all I have so I can rot in poverty, while someone else stuffs themselves on my money?

MICHELE: I do not exactly want that. But I'm thinking: what if the workers profiting from their numbers and basing themselves on your theory that life is a struggle and that rights derive from facts, get the idea into their heads of creating a new "historic fact", by taking away your land and capital and inaugurating new rights?

PROSPERO: Ah! Certainly, that would complicate matters.

But... we shall continue on another occasion. Now I have to go to the theatre.

Good evening to you all.

TWO

AMBROGIO [*Magistrate*]: Listen, Signor Prospero, now that it is just between ourselves, all good conservatives. The other evening when you were talking to that empty head, Michele, I did not want to intervene; but, do you think that was the way to defend our institutions?

It very nearly seemed that you were the anarchist!

PROSPERO: Well, I never! Why is that?

AMBROGIO: Because, what you were saying in essence is that all of the present social organisation is founded on force, thereby providing arguments for those who would like to destroy it with force. But what about the supreme principles which govern civil societies, rights, morality, religion, don't they count for anything?

PROSPERO: Of course, you always have a mouth full of rights. It is a bad habit that comes from your profession.

If tomorrow the governments should decree, let's suppose, collectivism, you would condemn the supporters of private property with the same impassiveness with which today you condemn the anarchists... and always in the name of the supreme principles of eternal and immutable rights!

You see, it is only a question of names. You say rights, I say force; but, then, what really counts are the blessed *cara-binieri*, and whoever has them on their side is right.

AMBROGIO: Come, now, Signor Prospero! It seems impossible that your love of sophism must always stifle your conservative instincts.

You don't understand how many bad effects follow from the sight of a person such as yourself, one of the elders of the town, providing arguments for the worst enemies of order.

Believe me – we should stop this bad habit of squabbling among ourselves, at least in public; let's all unite to defend our institutions which because of the wickedness of the times are receiving some brutal blows ...and to look after our endangered interests.

PROSPERO: Let's unite, by all means; but if some strong measures are not taken, if you don't stop using liberal doctrines we will not resolve anything.

AMBROGIO: Oh! Yes, certainly. We need severe laws to be strictly applied.

But it is not enough. Force alone cannot keep a people subjected for long, particularly in this day and age. It is necessary to oppose propaganda with propaganda, there is a need to persuade people that we are right.

PROSPERO: You really are kidding yourself! My poor friend, in our common interest, I beg you, be careful of propaganda. It is subversive stuff even if it is carried out by conservatives; and your propaganda would always turn to the advantage of socialists, anarchists or whatever else they call themselves.

Go and persuade someone that is hungry that it is just that they don't eat, the more so when it is they who produce the food! So long as they don't think about it and continue to bless God and the boss for what little they receive, it's all right. But, from the moment they start to reflect on their position it's over: they will become an enemy with whom you will never be reconciled. Not on your life! We must avoid propaganda at all cost, stifle the printing press, with or without or perhaps, even against the law.

AMBROGIO: That's right, that's right.

PROSPERO: Prevent all meetings, dismantle all associations, send to jail all those who think...

CESARE [shopkeeper]: Easy, easy, don't let passion sweep you away. Remember that other governments, in more favourable times, adopted the measures that you are suggesting... and it precipitated their own downfall.

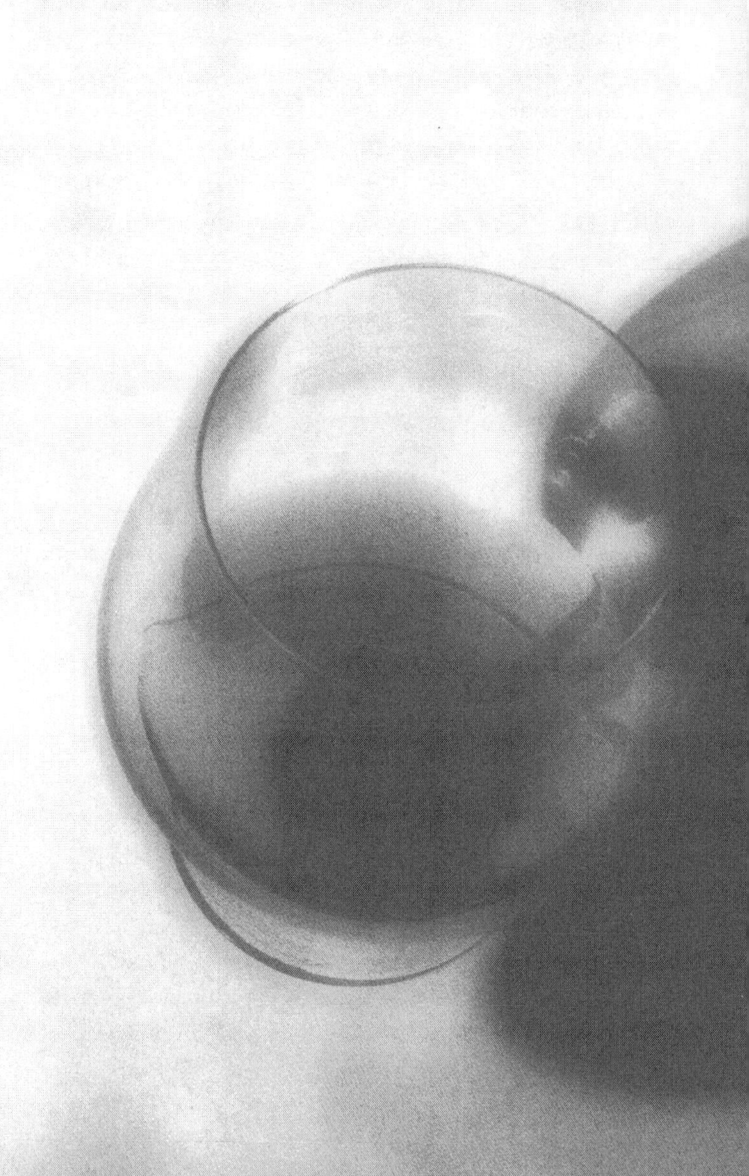

AMBROGIO: Hush, hush! Here comes Michele with an anarchist whom I sentenced last year to six months jail for a subversive manifesto. Actually, between ourselves, the manifesto was done in such a way that the law couldn't touch it, but, what can you do? The criminal intention was there... and, after all, society must be defended!

MICHELE: Good evening, Gentlemen. May I introduce to you an anarchist friend of mine who has accepted the challenge thrown down the other evening by Signor. Prospero.

PROSPERO: But, what challenge, what challenge?! We were only having a discussion among friends to pass the time.

However, you were explaining to us what anarchism is, which is something we have never been able to understand.

GIORGIO [*Anarchist*]: I am not a teacher of anarchism and I have not come to give a course on the subject; but I can, when needed, defend my ideas. Besides, there is a gentleman here (referring to the magistrate, Ambrogio, in an ironic tone) who ought to know more about it than I. He has condemned many people for anarchism; and since he is for a certainty a man of conscience, he would not have done so without first of all making a profound study of the arguments involved.

CESARE: Come, come, let's not get personal... and since we must speak of anarchism, let's start on the subject immediately.

You see, I also recognise that things are going badly and that remedies need to be found. But we don't need to become utopian, and above all we must avoid violence. Certainly, the government should take the workers' cause more to heart: it should provide work for the unemployed; protect the national industries, encourage commerce. But...

GIORGIO: How many things you would like this poor government to do! But the government does not want to become concerned for the interests of the workers, and it's understandable.

CESARE: How can it be understandable? Up to now, really, the government has shown a lack of capacity and perhaps little desire to remedy the ills of the country; but, tomorrow, enlightened and conscientious ministers might do what hasn't been done up to now.

GIORGIO: No, my dear sir, it is not a question of one ministry or another. It is a question of government in general; of all governments, those of today, like those of yesterday, and those of tomorrow. The government emanates from proprietors, it needs the support of proprietors to sustain itself, its members are themselves proprietors; how can it therefore serve the interest of workers?

On the other hand the government, even if it wanted to, could not resolve the social question because this is the product of general factors, that cannot be removed by a government and which in fact themselves determine the nature and the direction of government. In order to resolve the social question we must radically change the whole system which the government has the appointed mission of defending.

You talk about giving work to the unemployed. But, what can the government do if there is no work? Must it make people do useless work, and then who would pay them? Should it gear production to provide for the unsatisfied needs of the people? But, then, the proprietors would find themselves unable to sell the products which they expropriate from workers, as a matter of fact they would have to cease to be proprietors, since, the government in order to provide work for the people would take away from them the land and the capital which they have monopolised.

This would be social revolution, the liquidation of all of the past, and you well know that if this is not carried out by the workers, peasants and the underprivileged, the government will certainly never do it.

Protect industry and commerce you say: but the government is able, at the most, to favour one industrial class to the detriment of another, to favour the traders of one region at the expense of those of another, and so, in total, nothing would be gained, only a bit of favouritism, a bit of injustice and more unproductive expenditure. As far as a government which protects all, it is an absurd idea because governments do not produce anything and therefore can only transfer the wealth produced by others.

CESARE: But what then? If the government does not want, and is not able, to do anything, what remedy is there? Even if you make the revolution you will need to create another government; and since you say that all governments are the same, after the revolution everything will be the same as before.

GIORGIO: You would be right if our revolution produced simply a change of government. But we want the complete transformation of the property regime, of the system of production and exchange; and as far as the government is concerned, a useless, harmful and parasitic organ, we don't want one at all. We believe that while there is a government, in other words a body superimposed on society, and provided with the means to impose forcibly its own will, there will not be real emancipation, there will be no peace among people.

You know that I am an anarchist and anarchy means society without government.

CESARE: But what do you mean? A society without government! How would you be able to live? Who would make the law? Who would execute it?

GIORGIO: I see that you don't have any idea of what we want. In order to avoid time wasting digressions you must allow me to explain, briefly, but methodically, our programme; and then we can discuss matters to our mutual benefit.

But now it is late; we will continue next time.

THREE

CESARE: So tonight you will explain how we can live without government?

GIORGIO: I will do my best. But, first of all we must give some consideration to how things are in society as it is and whether it is really necessary to change its composition.

Looking at the society in which we live, the first phenomena that strike us are the poverty that afflicts the masses, the uncertainty of tomorrow which, more or less, weighs on everybody, the relentless struggle of everybody fighting everybody in order to conquer hunger...

AMBROGIO: But, my dear sir, you could go on talking for some time about these social evils; unfortunately, there are plenty of examples available. But, this does not serve any purpose, and it doesn't demonstrate that we would be better off by making everything topsy-turvy. It's not only poverty that afflicts humanity; there are also plagues, cholera, earthquakes... and it would be odd if you wished to direct the revolution against these courges.

Evil is in the nature of things...

GIORGIO: But in fact I want to demonstrate to you that poverty depends on the present mode of social organisation, and that in a more egalitarian and rationally organised society it must disappear.

When we do not know the causes of an evil and we don't have solutions, well, there is not much we can do about it; but as soon as the solution is found, it becomes everybody's concern and duty to put it into practice.

AMBROGIO: Here is your mistake: poverty results from causes superior to human will and human law. Poverty results from the meanness of nature which does not supply sufficient products to meet human desires.

Have a look at animals, where you cannot blame *capitalist infamy* nor *tyrannical government*; they must fight for food and often die of hunger.

When the cupboard's bare, the cupboard's bare. The truth is that there are too many people in the world. If people were able to control themselves and did not have children unless they could maintain them... Have you read Malthus?

GIORGIO: Yes, a little; but it's all the same if I hadn't read his work. What I know, without needing to read any part of it, is that you must have some nerve, I must say to maintain such things!

Poverty results from meanness of nature, you say, even though you are aware that there is uncultivated land...

AMBROGIO: If there is uncultivated land it means that it cannot be cultivated, that it cannot produce enough to pay for the costs involved.

GIORGIO: You believe that?

Try an experiment and give it to the peasants and you will see what gardens they'll create. But, you are not serious? Why, much of this land was cultivated in times when the art of agriculture was in its infancy and chemistry and agricultural technology hardly existed! Don't you know that today even stones can be transformed into fertile land? Don't you know that agronomists, even the less visionary ones, have calculated that a territory like Italy, if rationally cultivated could easily maintain in plenty a population of one hundred million?

The real reason why land is left uncultivated, and why cultivated land produces only a small proportion of its full potential, given the adoption of less primitive methods of cultivation, is because the proprietors do not have any interest in increasing its production.

They are not bothered about the welfare of the people; they produce in order to sell, and they know that when there is a lot of goods the prices are reduced and profit decreases and may end up being, in total, less than when goods are scarce and can be sold at prices which suit them.

Not that this only happens in relation to agricultural products. In every branch of human activity it is the same. For instance: in every city the poor are forced to live in infected hovels, crowded together without any regard for hygiene or morals, in conditions in which it is impossible to keep clean and achieve a human existence. Why does this happen? Perhaps because there are no houses? But why aren't sound, comfortable and beautiful houses built for everybody?

The stones, bricks, lime, steel, timber, all the materials needed for construction exist in abundance; as do the unemployed bricklayers, carpenters, and architects who ask for nothing more than to work; why, then, is there so much idle capacity when it could be utilised to everybody's advantage.

The reason is simple, and it is that, if there were a lot of houses, the rents would go down. The proprietors of the houses already built, who are the same people who have the means to build others, don't really have any desire to see their rents decrease just to win the approval of the poor.

CESARE: There is some truth in what you are saying; but you are deceiving yourself about the explanation for the painful things that are afflicting our country.

The cause of the land being badly cultivated or left idle, of business running aground, and of poverty in general is the lack of *élan* in the bourgeoisie. Capitalists are either fearful or ignorant, and don't want or don't know how to develop industries; the landowners don't know how to break with their grandfathers' methods and don't want to be bothered; traders don't know how to find new outlets and the government with its fiscal policy and its stupid customs policy instead of encouraging private initiatives, obstructs and suffocates them in their infancy. Have a look at France, England and Germany.

GIORGIO: That our bourgeoisie is indolent and ignorant I don't doubt, but its inferiority only supplies the explanation for why it is beaten by the bourgeoisie of other countries in the struggle to conquer the world market: it does not in any way supply the reason for people's poverty. And the clear evidence is that poverty, the lack of work and all the rest of the social evils exist in countries where the bourgeoisie is more active and more intelligent, as much as they do in Italy; actually, those evils are generally more intense in countries where industry is more developed, unless the workers have been able, through organisation, resistance or rebellion, to acquire better living conditions.

Capitalism is the same everywhere. In order to survive and prosper it needs a permanent situation of partial scarcity: it needs it to maintain its prices and to create hungry masses to work under any conditions.

You see, in fact, when production is in full swing in a country it is never to give producers the means to increase consumption, but always for sales to an external market. If the domestic consumption increases it occurs only when the workers have been able to profit from these circumstances to demand an increase in their wages and as a consequence

have been enabled to buy more goods. But then, when for one reason or another the external market for which they produce does not buy anymore, crisis comes, work stops, wages decline and dire poverty begins to cause havoc again. And yet, in this same country where the great majority lacks everything, it would be so much more reasonable to work for their own consumption! But, then, what would the capitalists gain out of that!

AMBROGIO: So, you think it is all the fault of capitalism?

GIORGIO: Yes of course; or more generally it's due to the fact that a few individuals have hoarded the land and all the instruments of production and can impose their will on the workers, in such a fashion that instead of producing to satisfy people's needs and with these needs in view, production is geared towards making a profit for the employers.

All the justifications you think up to preserve bourgeois privileges are completely erroneous, or so many lies. A little while ago you were saying that the cause of poverty is the scarcity of products. On another occasion, confronting the problems of the unemployed, you would have said that the warehouses are full, that the goods cannot be sold, and that the proprietors cannot create employment in order to throw goods away.

In fact this typifies the absurdity of the system: we die of hunger because the warehouses are full and there is no need to cultivate land, or rather, the landowners don't need their land cultivated; shoemakers don't work and thus walk about in worn out shoes because there are too many shoes.. and so it goes...

AMBROGIO: So it is the capitalists who should die of hunger?

GIORGIO: Oh! Certainly not. They should simply work like everybody else. It might seem harsh to you, but you don't understand: when one eats well work is no longer threatening. I can show you in fact you that it is a need and a fulfilment of human nature. But be fair, tomorrow I have to go to work and it is already very late.

Until next time.

FOUR

CESARE: I like arguing with you. You have a certain way of putting things that makes you appear correct... and, indeed, I am not saying that you are completely in the wrong.

There are certainly some absurdities, real or apparent, in the present social order. For example, I find it difficult to understand the customs policy. While here people are dying of hunger or associated diseases because they lack sufficient bread of good quality, the government makes it difficult to import grain from America, where they have more than they need and would like nothing better than to sell it to us. It's like being hungry but not wishing to eat!

However...

GIORGIO: Yes indeed, but the government is not hungry; and neither are the large wheat growers of Italy, in whose interests the government places the duty on wheat. If those who are hungry were free to act, you would see that they would not reject the wheat!

CESARE: I know that and I understand that with these sorts of arguments you make the common people, who only see things in broad terms and from one point of view, disaffected. But in order to avoid mistakes we must look at all sides of the question, as I was on the point of doing when you interrupted me.

It is true that the proprietors' interests greatly influence the imposition of an import tax. But on the other hand, if there was open entry, the Americans, who can produce wheat and meat in more favourable conditions than ours, would end up supplying the whole of our market: and what would our farmers do then? The proprietors would be ruined, but the workers would fare even worse. Bread would sell for small amounts of money. But if there was no way of earning that money you would still die of hunger. And, then the Americans, whether the goods are dear or cheap, want to get paid, and if in Italy we don't produce, with what are we going to pay?

You could say to me that in Italy we could cultivate those products suited to our soil and climate and then exchange them abroad: wine for instance, oranges, flowers and the like. But what if the things that we are capable of producing on favourable terms are not wanted by others, either because they have no use for them or because they produce them themselves? Not to mention that to change the production regime you need capital, knowledge and above all time: what would we eat in the meantime?

GIORGIO: Perfect! You have put your finger on it. Free trade cannot solve the question of poverty any more than protectionism. Free trade is good for consumers and harms the producers, and vice versa, protectionism is good for the protected producers but does harm to consumers; and since workers are at the same time both consumers and producers, in the end it is always the same thing.

And it will always be the same until the capitalist system is abolished.

If workers worked for themselves, and not for the owner's profits, then each country would be able to produce sufficient for its own needs, and they would only have to come to an agreement with other countries to distribute productive work according to the soil quality, climate, the availability of resources, the inclinations of the inhabitants etc. in order that all men should enjoy the best of everything with the minimum possible effort.

CESARE: Yes, but these are only pipe dreams.

GIORGIO: They may be dreams today; but when the people have understood how they could improve life, the dream would soon be transformed into reality. The only stumbling blocks are the egoism of some and the ignorance of others.

CESARE: There are other obstacles, my friend. You think that once the proprietors are thrown out you would wallow in gold...

GIORGIO: That is not what I'm saying. On the contrary, I think that to overcome this condition of scarcity in which capitalism maintains us, and to organise production largely to satisfy the needs of all, you need to do a lot of work; but it is not even the willingness to work that people lack, it is the possibility. We are complaining about the present system not so much because we have to maintain some idlers: even though this certainly does not please us – but, because it is these idlers that regulate work and prevent us from working in good conditions and producing an abundance for all.

CESARE: You exaggerate. It is true that often proprietors don't employ people in order to speculate on the scarcity of products, but more often it is because they themselves lack capital.

Land and raw materials are not enough for production. You need, as you know, tools, machinery, premises, the means to pay the workers while they work, in a word, capital; and this only accumulates slowly. How many ventures fail to get off the ground, or, having got off the ground, fail due to a shortage of capital! Can you imagine the effect then if, as you desire, a social revolution came about? With the destruction of capital, and the great disorder that would follow it, a general impoverishment would result.

GIORGIO: This is another error, or another lie from the defenders of the present order: the shortage of capital.

Capital may. be lacking in this or that undertaking because it has been cornered by others; but if we take society as a whole, you'll find that there is a great quantity of inactive capital, just as there is a great quantity of uncultivated land.

Don't you see how many machines are rusting, how many factories remain closed, how many houses there are without tenants.

There is a need for food to nourish workers while they work; but really workers must eat even if they are unemployed. They eat little and badly, but they remain alive and are ready to work as soon as an employer has need of them. So, it is not because there is a lack of the means of subsistence that workers don't work; and if they could work on their own account, they would adapt themselves, where it was really necessary, to work while living just as they do when they are unemployed, because they would know that with this temporary sacrifice they could then finally escape from the social condition of poverty and subjection.

Imagine, and this is something that has been witnessed many times, that an earthquake destroys a city ruining an entire district. In a little time the city is reconstructed in a form more beautiful than before and not a trace of the disaster remains. Because in such a case it is in the interests of proprietors and capitalists to employ people, the means are quickly found, and in the blink of an eye an entire city is reconstructed, where before they had continually asserted that they lacked the means to build a few "workers' houses".

As far as the destruction of capital that would take place at the time of the revolution, it is to be hoped that as part of a conscious movement that has as its aim the common ownership of social wealth, the people would not want to destroy what is to become their own. In any case it would not be as bad as an earthquake!

No – there will certainly be difficulties before things work out for the best; but, I can only see two serious obstacles, which must be overcome before we can begin: people's lack of consciousness and… the *carabinieri.*

AMBROGIO: But, tell me a little more; you talk of capital, work, production, consumption etc.; but you never talk of rights, justice, morals and religion?

The issues of how to best utilise land and capital are very important; but more important still are the moral questions. I also would like everybody to live well, but if in order to reach this utopia we have to violate moral laws, if we have to repudiate the eternal principles of right, upon which every civil society should be founded, then I would infinitely prefer that the sufferings of today went on forever!

And then, just think that there must also be a supreme will that regulates the world. The world did not come into being on its own and there must be *something beyond it* – I am not saying God, Paradise, Hell, because you would be quite capable of not believing in them – there must be *something beyond* this world that explains everything and where one finds compensation for the apparent injustices down here.

Do you think you can violate this pre-established harmony of the universe? You are not able to do so. We cannot do other than yield to it.

For once stop inciting the masses, stop giving rise to fanciful hopes in the souls of the least fortunate, stop blowing on the fire that is unfortunately smouldering beneath the ashes.

Would you, or other modern barbarians, wish to destroy in a terrible social cataclysm the civilization that is the glory of our ancestors and ourselves? If you want to do something worthwhile, if you want to relieve as much as possible the suffering of the poor, tell them to resign themselves to their fate, because true happiness lies in being contented. After all, everyone carries their own cross; every class has its own tribulations and duties, and it is not always those who live among riches that are the most happy.

GIORGIO: Come, my dear magistrate, leave aside the declarations about "grand principles" and the conventional indignation; we are not in court here, and, for the moment, you do not have to pronounce any sentence on me.

How would one guess, from hearing you talk, that you are not one of the underprivileged! And how useful is the resignation of the poor... for those who live off them.

First of all, I beg you, leave aside the transcendental and religious arguments, in which even you don't believe. Of mysteries of the Universe I know nothing, and you know no more; so it is pointless to bring them into the discussion. For the rest, be aware that the belief in a supreme maker, in God the creator and father of humanity would not be a secure weapon for you. If the priests, who have always been and remain in the service of the wealthy, deduce from it that it is the duty of the poor to resign themselves to their fate, others can deduce (and in the course of history have so deduced) the right to justice and equality. If God is our common father then we are all related. God cannot want some of his children to exploit and martyr the others; and the rich, the rulers, would be so many Cains cursed by the Father.

But, let's drop it.

AMBROGIO: Well then, let's forget about religion if you wish since so much of it would be pointless to you. But you would acknowledge rights, morals, a superior justice!

GIORGIO: Listen: if it is true that rights, justice and morals may require and sanction oppression and unhappiness, even of only one human being, I would immediately say to you, that rights, justice and morals are only lies, infamous weapons forged to defend the privileged; and such they are when they mean what you mean by them.

Rights, justice, morals should aim at the maximum possible good for all, or else they are synonyms for arrogant behaviour and injustice. And, it is certainly true that this conception of them answers to the necessities of existence and the development of human social cooperation, that has formed and persisted in the human conscience and continually gains in strength, in spite of all the opposition from those who up to now have dominated the world. You yourself could not defend, other than with pitiful sophism, the present social institutions with your interpretation of abstract principles of morality and justice.

AMBROGIO: You really are very presumptuous. It is not enough to deny, as it seems to me you do, the right to property, but you maintain that we are incapable of defending it with our own principles...

Giorgio: Yes, precisely: If you wish I will demonstrate it to
you next time.

FIVE

GIORGIO: Well then, my dear magistrate, if I am not mistaken, we were talking about the right to property.

AMBROGIO: Indeed. I am really curious to hear how you would defend, in the name of justice and morals, your proposals for despoliation and robbery.

A society in which no-one is secure in their possessions would no longer be a society, but a horde of wild beasts ready to devour each other.

GIORGIO: Doesn't it seem to you that this is precisely the case with today's society?

You are accusing us of despoliation and robbery; but on the contrary, isn't it the proprietors who continually despoil the workers and rob them of the fruits of their labour?

AMBROGIO: Proprietors use their goods in ways they believe for the best, and they have the right to do so, in the same way the workers freely dispose of their labour. Owners and workers contract freely for the price of work, and when the contract is respected no one can complain.

Charity can relieve acute troubles, unmerited troubles, but rights must remain untouchable.

GIORGIO: But you are speaking of a free contract! The worker who does not work cannot eat, and his liberty resembles that of a traveller, assaulted by thieves, who gives up his purse for fear of losing his life.

AMBROGIO: All right; but you cannot use this to negate the right of each person to dispose of their property as they see fit.

GIORGIO: Their property, their property! But doesn't this come about because the landowners are able to claim that the land and its produce as theirs and the capitalists are able to claim as theirs the instruments of labour and other capital created by human activity?

AMBROGIO: The law recognizes their right to it.

GIORGIO: Ah! If it is only the law, then even a street assassin could claim the right to assassinate and to rob: he would only have to formulate a few articles of law that recognised these rights. On the other hand, this is precisely what the dominant class has accomplished: it has created laws to legitimize the usurpations that it has already perpetrated, and has made them a means of new appropriations.

If all your "supreme principles" are based on the codes of law, it will be enough if tomorrow there is a law decreeing the abolition of private property, and that which today you call robbery and despoliation would instantly become a "supreme principle".

AMBROGIO: Oh! But the law must be just! It must conform to the principles of rights and morality, and should not be the result of unbridled whims, or else...

GIORGIO: So, it's not the law that creates rights, but rights which justify law. Then by what right does all the existing wealth, both natural wealth, and that created by the work of humanity belong to a few individuals and gives them the right of life and death over the masses of the underprivileged?

AMBROGIO: It is the right that every person has, and must have, to dispose freely of the product of their activity. It is natural to humanity, without it civilisation would not have been possible.

GIORGIO: Well, I never! Here we now have a defender of the rights of labour. Bravo, really! But tell me, how come those who work are those who have nothing, while property actually belongs to those who don't work?

Doesn't it occur to you that the logical outcome of your theory is that the present proprietors are thieves and that, in justice, we need to expropriate them in order to give the wealth which they have usurped to its legitimate owners, the workers?

AMBROGIO: If there are some proprietors who do not work it is because they were the first to work, they or their ancestors, and had the merit to save and the genius to make their savings bear fruit.

GIORGIO: Indeed, can you imagine a worker, who as a rule, earns scarcely enough to keep himself alive, saving and putting together some wealth!

You know very well that the origin of property is violence, robbery and theft, legal or illegal. But, let's assume if you like that someone has made some economies of production in his work, his own personal work: if he wants to enjoy them later on, when and how he wishes, that is fine. But this view of things changes completely however when the process begins of making his savings, what you call, *bear fruit*. This means making others work and stealing from them a part of what they produce; it means hoarding some goods and selling them at a price higher than their cost; it means the artificial creation of scarcity in order to speculate upon it; it means taking away from others their livelihood derived from working freely in order to force them to work for poor wages; and many other similar things which do not correspond to a sense of justice and demonstrate that property, when it does not derive from straightforward and open robbery, derives from the work of others, which proprietors have, in one way or another, turned to their own advantage.

Does it seem just to you that a person who has, (let us concede), by their work and their genius put together a little capital, can because of this rob others of the products of their work, and furthermore bequeath to all the generations of his descendants the right to live in idleness on the backs of workers?

Does it seem just to you that, because there have been a few laborious and thrifty men – I say this to bring out your point – that have accumulated some capital, the great mass of humanity must be condemned to perpetual poverty and brutalisation?

And, on the other hand, even if someone had worked for themselves, with their muscles and their brains without exploiting anybody; even if, against all the odds, such a one had been able to produce much more than they needed without the direct or indirect cooperation of the society as a whole, it does not mean because of this that they should be authorised to do harm to others, to take away from others the means of existence. If someone built a road along the shore they could not, because of this, argue for a right to deny the access of others to the sea. If someone could till and cultivate on their own all the soil of a province, they could not presume because of this to starve all the inhabitants of that province. If someone had created some new and powerful means of production, they would not have the right to use their invention in such a way as to subject people to their rule and even less of bequeathing to the countless successions of their descendants the right to dominate and exploit future generations.

But I am losing my way to suppose for a moment that proprietors are workers or the descendants of workers! Would you like me to tell you the origin of the wealth of all the gentlemen in our community, both of noblemen of ancient stock as well as the *nouveaux riches*?

AMBROGIO: No, no, in charity, let's leave aside personal matters.

If there are some riches acquired by doubtful means this does not provide a reason to deny the right to property. The past is the past, and it's not useful to dig up old problems again.

GIORGIO: We'll leave them buried if that's what you want. As far as I am concerned it is not important. Individual property should be abolished, not so much because it has been acquired by more or less questionable means, as much as because it grants the right and the means to exploit the work of others, and its development will always end up making the great mass of people dependent on a few.

But, by the way, how can you justify individual landed property with your theory of savings? You can't tell me that this was produced from the work of the proprietors or of their ancestors?

AMBROGIO: You see. Uncultivated, sterile land has no value. People occupy it, reclaim it, make it yield, and naturally have a right to its crops, which wouldn't have been produced without their work on the land.

GIORGIO: All right: this is the right of the worker to the fruits of his own labour; but this right ceases when he ceases to cultivate the land. Don't you think so?

Now, how is it that the present proprietors possess territories, often immense, that they do not work, have never worked and most frequently do not allow others to work?

How is it that lands that have never been cultivated are privately owned? What is the work, what is the improvement which may have given a date of origin, in this case, to property rights?

The truth is that for land, even more than for the rest, the origin of private property, is violence. And you cannot successfully justify it, if you don't accept the principle that right equals force, and in that case... heaven help you if one day you become the most enfeebled.

AMBROGIO: But in short, you lose sight of social utility, the inherent necessity of civil society. Without the right to property there would be no security, no more orderly work: and society would dissolve in chaos.

GIORGIO: What! Now you talk of social utility? But when in our earlier conversations I only concerned myself with the damage produced by private property, you called me back to arguments about abstract rights!

Enough for this evening. Excuse me but I have to go. We'll go into it another time.

SIX

GIORGIO: Well, have you heard what has happened? Someone told a newspaper about the conversation that we had last time, and for having published it, the newspaper has been gagged.

AMBROGIO: Ah!

GIORGIO: Of course, it goes without saying you don't know anything...! I don't understand how you can claim to be so confident of your ideas when you are so afraid of the public hearing some discussion of them. The paper faithfully reported both your arguments and mine. You ought to be happy that the public is able to appreciate the rational basis upon which the present social constitution rests, and does justice to the futile criticisms of its adversaries. Instead you shut people up, you silence them.

AMBROGIO: I am not involved at all; I belong to the judicial magistracy and not to the public ministry.

GIORGIO: Yes, I know! But, you are colleagues all the same and the same spirit animates you all.

If my chatter annoys you, tell me... and I will go and chatter somewhere else.

AMBROGIO: No, no, on the contrary – I confess that I am interested. Let's continue; as regards the restraining order I will, if you like, put in a good word with the Public Prosecutor. After all, with the law as it is, no one is denied the right to discussion.

GIORGIO: Let's continue, then. Last time, if I remember rightly, in defending the right to property you took as the present basis positive law, in other words the civil code, then a sense of justice, then social utility. Permit me to sum up, in a few words, my ideas with respect to all this.

From my point of view individual property is unjust and immoral because it is founded either on open violence, on fraud, or on the legal exploitation of the labour of others; and it is harmful because it hinders production and prevents the needs of all being satisfied by what can be obtained from land and labour, because it creates poverty for the masses and generates hatred, crimes and most of the evils that afflict modern society.

For these reasons I would like to abolish it and substitute a property regime based on common ownership, in which all people, contributing their just amount of labour, will receive the maximum possible level of wellbeing.

AMBROGIO: Really, I can't see with what logic you have arrived at common property. You have fought against property because, according to you, it derives from violence and from the exploitation of the labour of others; you have said that capitalists regulate production with an eye to their profits and not the better to satisfy to the public need with the least possible effort of the workers; you have denied the right to obtain revenue from land which one has not cultivated oneself, to derive a profit from one's own money or to obtain interest by investing in the construction of houses and in other industries; but you have, however, recognised the right of workers to the products of their own labour, actually you have championed it. As a consequence, according to strict logic, on these criteria you can challenge the verification of the titles to property, and demand the abolition of interest on money and private income; you may even ask for the liquidation of the present society and the division of land and the instruments of labour among those who wish to use them... but you cannot talk of communism. Individual ownership of the products of one's labour must always exist; and, if you want your emancipated worker to have that security in the future without which no work will be done which does not produce an immediate profit, you must recognise individual ownership of the land and the instruments of production to the extent they are used.

GIORGIO: Excellent, please continue; we could say that even you are tarred with the pitch of socialism. You are of a socialist school different from mine, but it is still socialism. A socialist magistrate is an interesting phenomenon.

AMBROGIO: No, no, I'm no socialist. I was only demonstrating your contradictions and showing you that logically you should be a *mutualist* and not a communist, a supporter of the division of property.

And then I would have to say to you that the division of property into small portions would render any large enterprise impossible and result in general poverty.

GIORGIO: But I am not a mutualist, a partisan of the division of property, nor is, as far as I know, any other modern socialist.

I don't think that dividing property would be worse than leaving it whole in the hands of the capitalists; but I know that this division, where possible, would cause grave damage to production. Above all it could not survive and would lead again to the formation of great fortunes, and to the proletarianisation of the masses and, in the bitter end, to poverty and exploitation.

I say that *the worker has the right to the entire product of his work*: but I recognise that this right is only a formula of abstract justice; and means, in practice, that there should be no exploitation, that everyone must work and enjoy the fruits of their labour, according to the custom agreed among them.

Workers are not isolated beings that live by themselves and for themselves, but social beings that live in a continuous exchange of services with other workers, and they must coordinate their rights with those of the others. Moreover, it is impossible, the more so with modern production methods, to determine the exact labour that each worker contributed, just as it is impossible to determine the differences in productivity of each worker or each group of workers, how much is due to the fertility of the soil, the quality of the implements used, the advantages or difficulties flowing from the geographical situation or the social environment. Hence, the solution cannot be found in respect to the strict rights of each person, but must be sought in fraternal agreement, in solidarity.

AMBROGIO: But, then, there is no more liberty.

GIORGIO: On the contrary, it is only then that there will be liberty. You, so called liberals, call liberty the theoretical, abstract right to do something; and you would be capable of saying without smiling, or blushing, that a person who died of hunger because they were not able to procure food for themselves, was free to eat. We, on the contrary, call liberty the possibility of doing something – and this liberty, the only true one, becomes greater as the agreement among men and the support they give each other grows.

AMBROGIO: You said that if property were to be divided, the great fortunes would soon be restored and there would be a return to the original situation. Why is this?

GIORGIO: Because, at the beginning it would be an impossible goal to make everyone perfectly equal. There are different sorts of land, some produce a lot with little work and others a little with a lot of work; there are all sorts of advantages and disadvantages offered by different localities; there are also great differences in physical and intellectual strength between one person and another. Now, from these divisions rivalry and struggle would naturally arise: the best land, the best implements and the best sites would go to the strongest, the most intelligent or the most cunning. Hence, the best material means being in the hands of the most gifted people, they would quickly find themselves in a position superior to others, and starting from these early advantages, would easily grow in strength, thus commencing a new process of exploitation and expropriation of the weak, which would lead to the re-constitution of a bourgeois society.

AMBROGIO: So, really seriously, you are a communist? You want laws that would declare the share of each individual to be non-transferable and would surround the weak with serious legal guarantees.

GIORGIO: Oh! You always think that one can remedy anything with laws. You are not a magistrate for nothing. Laws are made and unmade to please the strongest.

Those who are a little stronger than the average violate them; those who are very much stronger repeal them, and make others to suit their interests.

AMBROGIO: And, so?

GIORGIO: Well then, I've already told you, it is necessary to substitute agreement and solidarity for struggle among people, and to achieve this it is necessary first of all to abolish individual property.

AMBROGIO: But there would be no problems with all the goodies available. Everything belongs to everybody, whoever wants to can work and who doesn't can make love; eat, drink, be merry! Oh, what a Land of Plenty! What a good life! What a beautiful madhouse! Ha! Ha! Ha!

GIORGIO: Considering the figure you are cutting by wanting to make a rational defence of a society that maintains itself with brute force, I don't really think that you have much to laugh about!

Yes my good sir, I am a communist. But you seem to have some strange notions of communism. Next time I will try and make you understand. For now, good evening.

SEVEN

AMBROGIO: Well, then, would you like to explain to us what this communism of yours is all about.

GIORGIO: With pleasure.

Communism is a method of social organisation in which people, instead of fighting among themselves to monopolise natural advantages and alternatively exploiting and oppressing each other, as happens in today's society, would associate and agree to cooperate in the best interest of all. Starting from the principle that the land, the mines and all natural forces belong to everybody, and that all the accumulated wealth and acquisitions of previous generations also belong to everybody, people, in communism, would want to work cooperatively, to produce all that is necessary.

AMBROGIO: I understand. You want, as was stated in a news-sheet that came to hand during an anarchist trial, *for each person to produce according to their ability and consume according to their needs; or, for each to give what they can and take what they need.* Isn't that so?

GIORGIO: In fact these are principles that we frequently repeat; but for them to represent correctly our conception of what a communist society would be like it is necessary to understand what is meant. It is not, obviously, about an absolute right to satisfy *all* of one's needs, because needs are infinite, growing more rapidly than the means to satisfy them, and so their satisfaction is always limited by productive capacity; nor would it be useful or just that the community in order to satisfy excessive needs, otherwise called caprices, of a few individuals, should undertake work, out of proportion to the utility being produced. Nor are we talking about employing *all* of one's strength in producing things, because taken literally, this would mean working until one is exhausted, which would mean that by maximising the satisfaction of human needs we destroy humanity.

What we would like is for everybody to live in the best possible way: so that everybody with a minimum amount of effort will obtain maximum satisfaction. I don't know how to give you a theoretical formula which correctly depicts such a state of affairs; but when we get rid of the social environment of the boss and the police, and people consider each other as family, and think of helping instead of exploiting one another, the practical formula for social life will soon be found. In any case, we will make the most of what we know and what we can do, providing for piece-by-piece modifications as we learn to do things better.

AMBROGIO: I understand: you are a partisan of the *prise au tas*, as your comrades from France would say, that is to say each person produces what he likes and *throws in the heap*, or, if you prefer, brings to the communal warehouse what he has produced; and each *takes from the heap* whatever he likes and whatever he needs. Isn't that so?

GIORGIO: I notice that you decided to inform yourself a little about this issue, and I guess that you have read the trial documents more carefully than you normally do when you send us to jail. If all magistrates and policemen did this, the things that they steal from us during the searches would at least be useful for something!

But, let's return to our discussion. Even this formula of *take from the heap* is only a form of words, that expresses an inclination to substitute for the market spirit of today the spirit of fraternity and solidarity, but it doesn't indicate with any certainty a definite method of social organisation. Perhaps you could find among us some who take that formula literally, because they suppose that work undertaken spontaneously would always be abundant and that products would accumulate in such quantity and variety that rules about work or consumption would be pointless. But I don't think like that: I believe, as I've told you, that humans always have more needs than the means to satisfy them and I am glad of it because this is a spur to progress; and I think that, even if we could, it would be an absurd waste of energy to produce blindly to provide for all possible needs, rather than calculating the actual needs and organising to satisfy them with as little effort as possible. So, once again, the solution lies in accord between people and in the agreements, expressed or silent, that will come about when they have achieved equality of conditions and are inspired by a feeling of solidarity.

Try to enter into the spirit of our programme, and don't worry overmuch about formulas that, in our party just like any other, are not pithy and striking but are always a vague and inexact way of expressing a broad direction.

AMBROGIO: But don't you realise that communism is the negation of liberty, and of human personality? Perhaps, it may have existed in the beginning of humanity, when human beings, scarcely developed intellectually and morally, were happy when they could satisfy their material appetites as members of the horde. Perhaps it is possible in a religious society, or a monastic order, that seeks the suppression of human passion, and prides itself on the incorporation of the individual into the religious community and claims obedience to be a prime duty. But in a modern society, in which there is a great flowering of civilization produced by the free activity of individuals, with the need for independence and liberty that torments and ennobles modern man, communism is not an impossible dream, it is a return to barbarism. Every activity would be paralysed; every promising contest where one could distinguish oneself, assert one's own individuality, extinguished...

GIORGIO: And so on, and so on.

Come on. Don't waste your eloquence. These are well-known stock phrases... and are no more than a lot of brazen and irresponsible lies. Liberty, individuality of those who die of hunger! What crude irony! What profound hypocrisy!

You defend a society in which the great majority lives in bestial conditions, a society in which workers die of privation and of hunger, in which children die by the thousands and millions for lack of care, in which women prostitute themselves because of hunger, in which ignorance clouds the mind, in which even those who are educated must sell their talent and lie in order to eat, in which nobody is sure of tomorrow – and you dare talk of liberty and individuality?

Perhaps, liberty and the possibility of developing one's own individuality exist for you, for a small caste of privileged people.. and perhaps not even for them. These same privileged persons are victims of the struggle between one human being and another that pollutes all social life, and they would gain substantially if they were able to live in a society of mutual trust, free among the free, equal among equals.

However can you maintain the view that solidarity damages liberty and the development of the individual? If we were discussing the family – and we will discuss it whenever you want – you could not fail to let loose one of the usual conventional hymns to that holy institution, that foundation stone etc. etc. Well, in the family – what is it we extol, if not that which generally exists – the love and solidarity prevailing among its members. Would you maintain that the various family members would be freer and their individuality more developed if instead of loving each other and working together for the common good, they were to steal, hate and hit one another?

AMBROGIO: But to regulate society like a family, to organise and to make a communist society function, you need an immense centralisation, an iron despotism, and an omnipresent state. Imagine what oppressive power a government would have that could dispose of all social wealth and assign to everyone the work they must do and the goods they could consume!

GIORGIO: Certainly if communism was to be what you imagine it to be and how it is conceived by a few authoritarian schools then it would be an impossible thing to achieve, or, if possible, would end up as a colossal and very complex tyranny, that would then inevitably provoke a great reaction.

But there is none of this in the communism that we want. We want free communism, *anarchism*, if the word doesn't offend you. In other words, we want a communism which is freely organised, from bottom to top, starting from individuals that unite in associations which slowly grow bit by bit into ever more complex federations of associations, finally embracing the whole of humanity in a general agreement of cooperation and solidarity. And just as this communism will be freely, constituted, it must freely maintain itself through the will of those involved.

AMBROGIO: But for this to become possible you would need human beings to be angels, for everyone to be altruists! Instead people are by nature egoistical, wicked, hypocritical and lazy.

GIORGIO: Certainly, because for communism to become possible there is a need that human beings, partly because of an impulse toward sociability and partly from a clear understanding of their interests, don't bear each other ill-will but want to get on and to practice mutual aid. But this state, far from seeming an impossibility, is even now normal and common. The present social organisation is a permanent cause of antagonism and conflict between classes and individuals: and if despite this society is still able to maintain itself and doesn't literally degenerate into a pack of wolves devouring each other, it is precisely because of the profound human instinct for society that produces the thousand acts of solidarity, of sympathy, of devotion, of sacrifice that are carried out every moment, without them even being thought about, that makes possible the continuance of society, notwithstanding the causes of disintegration that it carries within itself.

Human beings are, by nature, both egoistic and altruistic, biologically pre-determined I would say prior to society. If humans had not been egoistic, if, that is to say, they had not had the instinct of self-preservation, they could not have existed as individuals; and if they hadn't been altruistic, in other words if they hadn't had the instinct of sacrificing themselves for others, the first manifestation of which one finds in the love of one's children, they could not have existed as a species, nor, most probably, have developed a social life.

The coexistence of the egoistic and the altruistic sentiment and the impossibility in existing society of satisfying both ensures that today no one is satisfied, not even those who are in privileged positions. On the other hand communism is the social form in which egoism and altruism mingle – and every person will accept it because it benefits everybody.

AMBROGIO: It may be as you say: but do you think that everybody would want and would know how to adapt themselves to the duties that a communist society imposes, if, for instance, people do not want to work? Of course, you have an answer for everything in theory, as best suits your argument, and you will tell me that work is an organic need, a pleasure, and that everybody will compete to have as much as possible of such a pleasure!

GIORGIO: I am not saying that, although I know that you would find that many of my friends who would say so. According to me what is an organic need and a pleasure is movement, nervous and muscular activity; but work is a disciplined activity aimed at an objective goal, external to the organism. And I well understand how it is that one may prefer horse-riding when, instead it is necessary to plant cabbages. But, I believe that human beings, when they have an end in view, can adapt and do adapt to the conditions necessary to achieve it.

Since the products that one obtains through work are necessary for survival, and since nobody will have the means to force others to work for them, everyone will recognise the necessity of working and will favour that structure in which work will be less tiring and more productive, and that is, in my view, a communist organisation.

Consider also that in communism these same workers organise and direct work, and therefore have every interest in making it light and enjoyable; consider that in communism there will naturally develop a public view that will condemn idleness as damaging to all, and if there will be some loafers, they will only be an insignificant minority, which could be tolerated without any perceptible harm.

AMBROGIO: But suppose that in spite of your optimistic forecasts there should be a great number of loafers, what would you do? Would you support them? If so, then you might as well support those whom you call the bourgeoisie!

GIORGIO: Truly there is a great difference; because the bourgeois not only take part of what we produce, but they prevent us from producing what we want and how we want to produce it. Nonetheless I am by no means saying that we should maintain idlers, when they are in such numbers as to cause damage: I am very afraid that idleness and the habit of living off others may lead to a desire to command. Communism is a free agreement: who doesn't accept it or maintain it, remains outside of it.

AMBROGIO: But then there will be a new underprivileged class?

GIORGIO: Not at all. Everyone has the right to land, to the instruments of production and all the advantages that human beings can enjoy in the state of civilization that humanity has reached. If someone does not want to accept a communist life and the obligation that it supposes, it is their business. They and those of a like mind will come to an agreement, and if they find themselves in a worse state than the others this will prove to them the superiority of communism and will impel them to unite with the communists.

AMBROGIO: So therefore one will be free·not to accept communism?

GIORGIO: Certainly: and whoever it is, will have the same rights as the communists over the natural wealth and accumulated products of previous generations. For heaven's sake!! I have always spoken of free agreement, of free communism. How could there be liberty without a possible alternative?

AMBROGIO: So, you don't want to impose your ideas with force?

GIORGIO: Oh! Are you crazy? Do you take us for policemen or magistrates?

AMBROGIO: Well, there is nothing wrong then. Everyone is free to pursue their dream!

GIORGIO: Be careful not to make a blunder: to impose ideas is one thing, to defend oneself from thieves and violence, and regain one's rights is something else.

AMBROGIO: Ah! Ah! So to *regain your rights* you would use force, is that right?

GIORGIO: To this I won't give you an answer: it may be useful to you in putting together a bill of indictment in some trial. What I will tell you is that certainly, when the people have become conscious of their rights and want to put an end to... you will run the risk of being treated rather roughly. But this will depend on the resistance that you offer. If you give up with good will, everything will be peaceful and amiable; if on the contrary you are pig-headed, and I'm sure that you will be, so much the worse for you. Good evening.

EIGHT

AMBROGIO: You know! The more I think about your free communism the more I am persuaded that you are ...a true original.

GIORGIO: And why is that?

AMBROGIO: Because you always talk about work, enjoyment, accords, agreements, but you never talk of social authority, of government. Who will regulate social life? Who will be the government? How will it be constituted? Who will elect it? By what means will it ensure that laws are respected and offenders punished? How will the various powers be constituted, legislative, executive or judicial?

GIORGIO: We don't know what to do with all these powers of yours. We don't want a government. Are you still not aware that I am an anarchist?

AMBROGIO: Well, I've told you that you are an original. I could still understand communism and admit that it might be able to offer great advantages, if everything were to be still regulated by an enlightened government, which had the strength to make everybody have a respect for the law. But like this, without government, without law! What kind of muddle would there be?

GIORGIO: I had foreseen this: first you were against communism because you said that it needed a strong and centralised government; now that you have heard talk of a society without government, you would even accept communism, so long as there was a government with an iron fist. In short, it is liberty which scares you most of all!

AMBROGIO: But this is to jump out of the frying pan into the fire! What is certain is that a society without a government cannot exist. How would you expect things to work, without rules, without regulations of any kind? What will happen is that someone will steer to the right, somebody else to the left and the ship will remain stationary, or more likely, go to the bottom.

GIORGIO: I did not say that I do not want rules and regulations. I said to you that I don't want a *Government*, and by government I mean a power that makes laws and imposes them on everybody.

AMBROGIO: But if this government is elected by the people doesn't it represent the will of those same people? What could you complain about?

GIORGIO: This is simply a lie. A general, abstract, popular will is no more than a metaphysical fancy. The public is comprised of people, and people have a thousand different and varying wills according to variations in temperament and in circumstances, and expecting to extract from them, through the magic operation of the ballot box, a general will common to all is simply an absurdity. It would be impossible even for a single individual to entrust to somebody else the execution of their will on all the questions that could arise during a given period of time; because they themselves could not say in advance what would be their will on these various occasions. How could one speak for a collectivity, people, whose members at the very time of producing a mandate were already in disagreement among themselves?

Just think for a moment at the way elections are held – and note that, I intend speaking about the way they would work if all the people were educated and independent and thus the vote perfectly conscious and free. You, for instance, would vote for whoever you regard as best suited to serve your interests and to apply your ideas. This is already conceding a lot, because you have so many ideas and so many different interests that you would not know how to find a person that thinks always like you on all issues: but will it be then to such a person that you will give your vote and who will govern you? By no means. Your candidate might not be successful and so your will forms no part of the so called popular will: but let's suppose that they do succeed.

On this basis would this person be your ruler? Not even in your dreams. They would only be one among many (in the Italian parliament for instance one among 535) and you in reality will be ruled by a majority of people to whom you have never given your mandate. And this majority (whose members have received many different or contradictory mandates, or better still have received only a general delegation of power, without any specific mandate) unable, even if it wanted to, to ascertain a non-existent general will, and to make everybody happy, will do as it wishes, or will follow the wishes of those who dominate it at a particular moment.

Come on, it's better to leave aside this old-fashioned pretence of a government that represents the popular will.

There are certainly some questions of general order, about which at a given moment, all the people will agree. But, then, what is the point of government? When everybody wants something, they will only need to enact it.

AMBROGIO: Well in short, you have admitted that there is a need for rules, some norms for living. Who should establish them?

GIORGIO: The interested parties themselves, those who must follow these regulations.

AMBROGIO: Who would impose observance?

GIORGIO: No-one, because we are talking about norms which are freely accepted and freely followed. Don't confuse the norms of which I speak, that are practical conventions based on a feeling of solidarity and on the care that everyone must have for the collective interest, with the law which is a rule written by a few and imposed with force on everybody. We don't want laws, but free agreements.

AMBROGIO: And if someone violates the agreement?

GIORGIO: And why should someone violate an agreement with which they have has concurred? On the other hand, if some violations were to take place, they would serve as a notification that the agreement does not satisfy everybody and will have to be modified. And everybody will search for a better arrangement, because it is in everybody's interest that nobody is unhappy.

AMBROGIO: But it seems that you long for a primitive society in which everyone is self-sufficient and the relations between people are few, basic and restricted.

GIORGIO: Not at all. Since from the moment that social relations multiply and become more complex, humanity experiences greater moral and material satisfaction, we will seek relationships as numerous and complex as possible.

AMBROGIO: But then you will need to delegate functions, to give out tasks, to nominate representatives in order to establish agreements.

GIORGIO: Certainly. But don't think that this is equivalent to nominating a government. The government makes laws and enforces them, while in a free society delegation of power is only for particular, temporary tasks, for certain jobs, and does not give rights to any authority nor any special reward. And the resolutions of the delegates are always subject to the approval of those they represent.

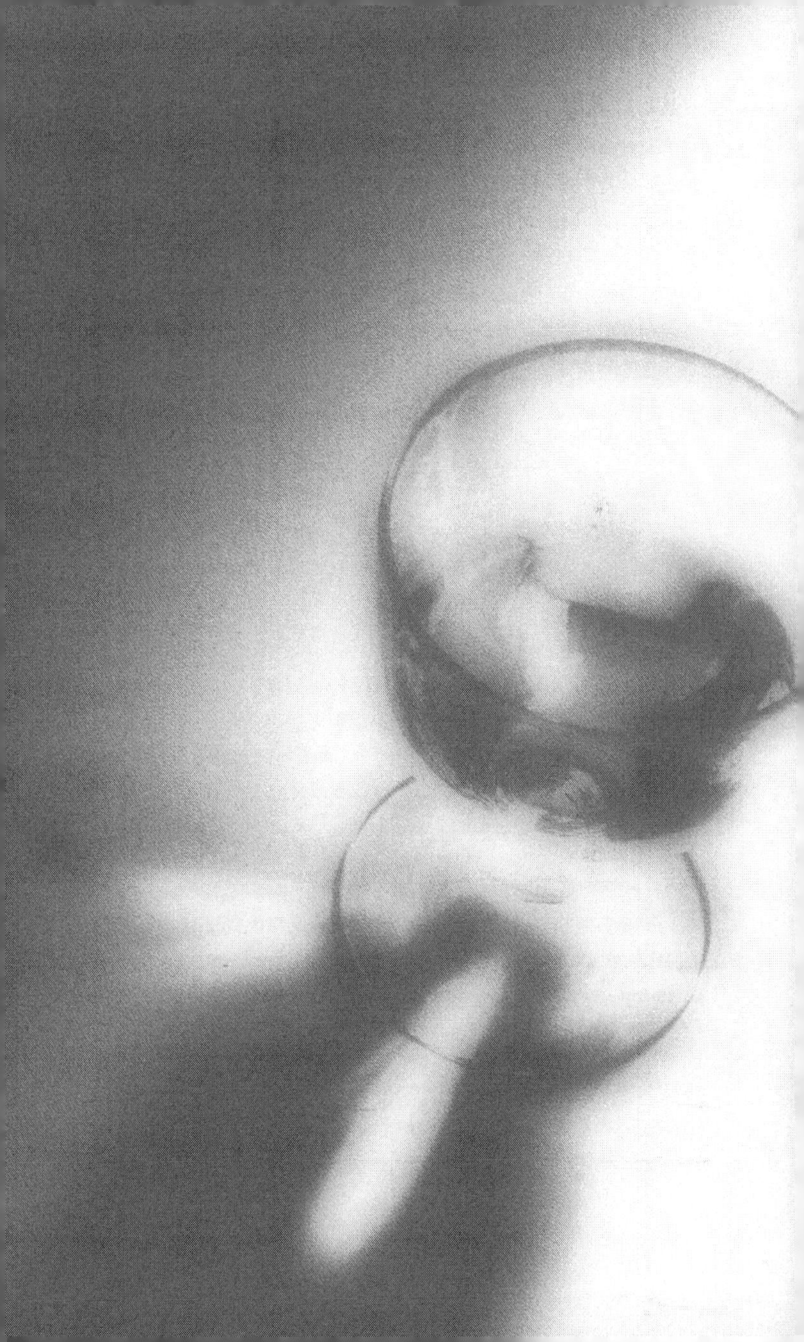

AMBROGIO: But you don't imagine that everyone will always agree. If there are some people that your social order does not suit, what will you do?

GIORGIO: Those people will make whatever arrangements best suit them, and we and they will reach an agreement to avoid bothering each other.

AMBROGIO: And if the others want to make trouble?

GIORGIO: Then... we will defend ourselves.

AMBROGIO: Ah! But don't you see that from this need for defence a new government might arise?

GIORGIO: Certainly I see it: and it is precisely because of this that I've always said that anarchism is not possible until the most serious causes of conflict are eliminated, a social accord serves the interests of all, and the spirit of solidarity is well developed among humanity.

If you want to create anarchism today, leaving intact individual property and the other social institutions that derive from it, such a civil war would immediately break out that a government, even a tyranny, would be welcomed as a blessing.

But if at the same time that you establish anarchism you abolish individual property, the causes of conflict that will survive will not be insurmountable and we will reach an agreement, because with agreement everyone will be advantaged.

After all, it is understood that institutions are only worth as much as the people that make them function – and anarchism in particular, that is the reign of free agreement, cannot exist if people do not understand the benefits of solidarity and don't want to agree.

That is why we engage in spreading propaganda.

NINE

AMBROGIO: Allow me to return to your anarchist communism. Frankly I cannot put up with it...

GIORGIO: Ah! I believe you. After having lived your life between codices and books of law in order to defend the rights of the State and those of the proprietors, a society without State and proprietors, in which there will no longer be any rebels and starving people to send to the galleys, must seem to you like something from another world.

But if you wish to set aside this attitude, if you have the strength to overcome your habits of mind and wish to reflect on this matter without bias, you would easily understand, that, allowing that the aim of society has to be the greatest well being for all, one necessarily arrives at anarchist communism as the solution. If you think on the contrary that society is made to engross a few pleasure loving individuals at the expense of the rest, well....

AMBROGIO: No, no, I admit that society must have as a goal the well-being of all, but I cannot because of this accept your system. I am trying hard to get inside your point of view, and since I have taken an interest in the discussion I would like, at least for myself, to have a clear idea of what you want: but your conclusions seem to be so utopian, so....

GIORGIO: But in short, what is it that you find obscure or unacceptable in the explanation that I have given you.

AMBROGIO: There is... I don't know... the whole system.

Let's leave aside the question of right, on which we will not agree; but let us suppose that, as you maintain, we all have an equal right to enjoy the existing wealth, I admit that communism would seem to be the most expeditious arrangement and perhaps the best. But, what seems to me absolutely impossible, is a society without government.

You build the whole of your edifice on the free will of the members of the association...

GIORGIO: Precisely.

AMBROGIO: And this is your error. Society means hierarchy, discipline, the submission of the individual to the collective. Without authority no society is possible.

GIORGIO: Exactly the reverse. A society in the strict sense of the word can only exist among equals; and these equals make agreements among themselves if in them they find pleasure and convenience, but they will not submit to each other.

Those relations of hierarchy and submission, that to you seem the essence of society, are relations between slaves and masters: and you would admit, I hope, that the slave is not really the partner of the master, just as a domestic animal is not the partner of the person who possesses it.

AMBROGIO: But do you truly believe in a society in which each person does what they want!

GIORGIO: On condition it's understood that people want to live in a society and therefore will adapt themselves to the necessities of social life.

AMBROGIO: And if they don't wish to?

GIORGIO: Then society would not be possible. But since it is only within society that humanity, at least in its modern form, can satisfy its material and moral needs, it is a strange supposition that we would wish to renounce what is the precondition of life and well being.

People have difficulty in coming to agreement when they discuss matters in abstract terms; but as soon as there is something to do, that must be done and which is of interest to everybody, as long as no one has the means to impose their will on others and to force them to do things their way, obstinacy and stubbornness soon cease, they become conciliatory, and the thing is done with the maximum possible satisfaction to everyone.

You must understand: nothing human is possible without the will of humanity. The whole problem for us lies in changing this will, that is to say it means making people understand that to war against each other, to hate each other, to exploit each other, is to lose everything, and persuading them to wish for a social order founded on mutual support and on solidarity.

AMBROGIO: So to bring about your anarchist communism you must wait until everybody is so persuaded, and has the will to make it work.

GIORGIO: Oh, no! We'd be kidding ourselves! Will is mostly determined by the social environment, and it is probable that while the present conditions last, the great majority will continue to believe that society cannot be organized in other ways from what now exists.

AMBROGIO: Well then?!

GIORGIO: So, we will create communism and anarchism among ourselves... when we are in sufficient numbers to do it – convinced that if others see that we are doing well for ourselves, they will soon follow suit. Or, at least, if we cannot achieve communism and anarchism, we will work to change social conditions in such a way as to produce a change of will in the desired direction.

You must understand; this is about a reciprocal interaction between the will and the surrounding social conditions... We are doing and will do whatever we can do so that we move towards our ideal.

What you must clearly understand is this. We do not want to coerce the will of anyone; but we do not want others to coerce our will nor that of the public. We rebel against that minority which through violence exploits and oppresses the people. Once liberty is won for ourselves and for all, and, it goes without saying, the means to be free, in other words the right to the use of land and of the instruments of production, we will rely solely on the force of words and examples to make our ideas triumph.

AMBROGIO: All right; and you think that in this way we will arrive at a society that governs itself simply through the voluntary agreement of its members? If that is the case it would be a thing without *precedent*!

GIORGIO: Not as much as you might think. As a matter of fact, in essence it has always been like that... that is if one considers the defeated, the dominated, the oppressed drawn from the lower levels of humanity, as not really part of society.

After all, even today the essential part of social life, in the dominant class as in the dominated class, is accomplished through spontaneous agreements, often unconscious, between individuals: by virtue of custom, points of honour, respect for promises, fear of public opinion, a sense of honesty, love, sympathy, rules of good manners – without any intervention by the law and the government. Law and governments become necessary only when we deal with relations between the dominators and the dominated. Among equals everyone feels ashamed to call a policeman, or have recourse to a judge!

In despotic States, where all the inhabitants are treated like a herd in the service of the sole ruler, no one has a will but the sovereign... and those whom the sovereign needs to keep the masses submissive. But, little by little as others arrive and achieve emancipation and enter the dominant class, that is society in the strict sense of the word, either through direct participation in government or by means of possessing wealth, society moulds itself in ways which satisfy the will of all the dominators. The whole legislative and executive apparatus, the whole government with its laws, soldiers, policemen, judges etc. serve only to regulate and ensure the exploitation of the people. Otherwise, the owners would find it simpler and more economical to agree among themselves and do away with the state. The bourgeois themselves have voiced the same opinion... when for a moment they forget that without soldiers and policemen the people would spoil the party.

Destroy class divisions, make sure that there are no more slaves to keep in check, and immediately the state will have no more reason to exist.

AMBROGIO: But don't exaggerate. The State also does things of benefit to all. It educates, watches over public health, defends the lives of citizens, organises public services... don't tell me that these are worthless or damaging things!

GIORGIO: Ugh! – Done the way the State usually does it, that is hardly at all. The truth is that it is always the workers who really do those things, and the State, setting itself up as their regulator, transforms such services into instruments of domination, turning them to the special advantage of the rulers and owners.

Education spreads, if there is in the public the desire for instruction and if there are teachers capable of educating; public health thrives, when the public knows, appreciates and can put into practice public health rules, and when there are doctors capable of giving people advice; the lives of citizens are safe when the people are accustomed to consider life and human liberties sacred and when... there are no judges and no police force to provide examples of brutality; public services will be organised when the public feels the need for them.

The State does not create anything: at best it is only other a superfluity, a worthless waste of energy. But if only it was just useless!

AMBROGIO: Leave it there. In any case I think you have said enough. I want to reflect upon it.

Until we meet again..

TEN

AMBROGIO: I have reflected on what you have been telling me during these conversations of ours... And I give up the debate. Not because I admit defeat; but... in a word, you have your arguments and the future may well be with you.

I am, in the meantime, a magistrate and as long as there is law, I must respect it and ensure that it is respected. You understand...

GIORGIO: Oh, I understand very well. Go, go if you like. It will be up to us to abolish the law, and so free you from the obligation to act against your conscience.

AMBROGIO: Easy, easy, I didn't say that... but, never mind.

I would like a few other explanations from you.

We could perhaps come to an understanding on the questions regarding the property regime and the political organisation of society; after all they are historic formations that have changed many times and possibly will change again. But there are some sacred institutions, some profound emotions of the human heart that you continually offend: the family, the fatherland!

For instance, you want to put everything in common. Naturally you will put even women in common, and thus make a great seraglio; isn't this so?

GIORGIO: Listen; if you want to have a discussion with me, please don't say foolish things and make jokes in bad taste. The question we are dealing with is too serious to interpose vulgar jokes!

AMBROGIO: But... I was serious. What would you do with the women?

GIORGIO: Then, so much the worse for you, because it is really strange that you don't understand the absurdity of what you have just said.

Put women in common! Why don't you say that we want to put men in common? The only explanation for this idea of yours is that you, through ingrained habit, consider woman as an inferior being made and placed on this world to serve as a domestic animal and as an instrument of pleasure for the male sex, and so you speak of her as if she were a thing, and imagine that we must assign her the same destiny as we assign to things.

But, we who consider woman as a human being equal to ourselves, who should enjoy all the rights and all the resources enjoyed by, or that ought to be enjoyed, by the male sex, find the question, "What will you do with the women?" empty of meaning. Ask instead: "What will the women do?" and I will answer that *they will do what they want to do*, and since they have the same need as men to live in a society, it is certain that *they will want* to come to agreements with their fellow creatures, men and women, in order to satisfy their needs to the best advantage for themselves and everybody else

AMBROGIO: I see; you consider women as equal to men. Yet many scientists, examining the anatomical structure and the physiological functions of the female body, maintain that woman is naturally inferior to man.

GIORGIO: Yes, of course. Whatever needs to be maintained, there is always a scientist willing to maintain it. There are some scientists that maintain the inferiority of women as there are others that, on the contrary, maintain that the understanding of women and their capacity for development are equal to that of men, and if today women generally appear to have less capacity than men this is due to the education they have received and the environment in which they live. If you search carefully you will even find some scientists, or at least women scientists, that assert that man is an inferior being, destined to liberate women from material toil and leave them free to develop their talents in an unlimited way. I believe that this view has been asserted in America.

But who cares. This is not about resolving a scientific problem, but about realising a vow, a human ideal.

Give to women all the means and the liberty to develop and what will come will come. If women are equal to men, or if they are more or less intelligent, it will show in practice – and even science will be advantaged, as it will have some positive data upon which to base its inductions.

AMBROGIO: So you don't take into consideration the faculties with which individuals are endowed?

GIORGIO: Not in the sense that these should create special rights. In nature you will not find two equal individuals; but we claim social equality for all, in other words the same resources, the same opportunities – and we think that this equality not only corresponds to the feelings of justice and fraternity that have developed in humanity, but works to the benefit of all, whether they are strong or weak.

Even among men, among males, there are some who are more and others who are less intelligent, but this does not mean that the one should have more rights than the other. There are some who hold that blondes are more gifted than brunettes or vice versa, that races with oblong skulls are superior to those with broad skulls or vice versa; and the issue, if it is based on real facts, is certainly interesting for science. But, given the current state of feelings and human ideals, it would be absurd to pretend that blondes and the dolichocephalic should command the browns and the branchycephalic or the other way round.

Don't you think so?

AMBROGIO: All right; but let's look at the question of the

family. Do you want to abolish it or organise it on another basis?

GIORGIO: Look. As far as the family is concerned we need to consider the economic relations, the sexual relations, and the relations between parents and children.

Insofar as the family is an economic institution it is clear that once individual property is abolished and as a consequence inheritance, it has no more reason to exist and will *de facto* disappear. In this sense, however, the family is already abolished for the great majority of the population, which is composed of proletarians.

AMBROGIO: And as far as sexual relations? Do you want free love, do...

GIORGIO: Oh, come on! Do you think that enslaved love could really exist? Forced cohabitation exists, as does feigned and forced love, for reasons of interest or of social convenience; probably there will be men and women who will respect the bond of matrimony because of religious or moral convictions; but true love cannot exist, cannot be conceived, if it is not perfectly free.

AMBROGIO: This is true, but if everyone follows the fancies inspired by the god of love, there will be no more morals and the world will become a brothel.

GIORGIO: As far as morals are concerned, you can really brag about the results of your institutions! Adultery, lies of every sort, long cherished hatreds, husbands that kill wives, wives that poison husbands, infanticide, children growing up amidst scandals and family brawls.... And this is the morality that you fear is being threatened by free love?

Today the world is a brothel, because women are often forced to prostitute themselves through hunger; and because matrimony, frequently contracted through a pure calculation of interest, is throughout the whole of its duration a union into which love either does not enter at all, or enters only as an accessory.

Assure everyone of the means to live properly and independently, give women the complete liberty to dispose of their own bodies, destroy the prejudices, religious and otherwise, that bind men and women to a mass of conventions that derive from slavery and which perpetuate it – and sexual unions will be made of love, and will give rise to the happiness of individuals and the good of the species.

AMBROGIO: But in short, are you in favour of lasting or temporary unions? Do you want separate couples, or a multiplicity and variety of sexual relations, or even promiscuity?

GIORGIO: We want liberty.

Up to now sexual relations have suffered enormously from the pressure of brutal violence, of economic necessity, of religious prejudices and legal regulations, that it has not been possible to work out what is the form of sexual relations which best corresponds to the physical and moral well being of individuals and the species.

Certainly, once we eliminate the conditions that today render the relations between men and women artificial and forced, a sexual hygiene and a sexual morality will be established that will be respected, not because of the law, but through the conviction, based on experience, that they satisfy our well being and that of the species. This can only come about as the effect of liberty.

AMBROGIO: And the children?

GIORGIO: You must understand that once we have property in common, and establish on a solid moral and material base the principle of social solidarity, the maintenance of the children will be the concern of the community, and their education will be the care and responsibility of everyone.

Probably all men and all women will love all the children; and if, as I believe is certain, parents have a special affection for their own children, they can only be delighted to know that the future of their children is secure, having for their maintenance and their education the cooperation of the whole society.

AMBROGIO: But, you do, at least, respect parents' rights over their children?

GIORGIO: Rights over children are composed of duties. One has many rights over them, that is to say many rights to guide them and to care for them, to love them and to worry about them: and since parents generally love their children more than anyone else, it is usually their duty and their right to provide for their needs. It isn't necessary to fear any challenges to this, because if a few unnatural parents give their children scant love and do not look after them they will be content that others will take care of the children and free them of the task.

If by a parent's rights over their children you mean the right to maltreat, corrupt and exploit them, then I absolutely reject those rights, and I think that no society worthy of the name would recognize and put up with them

AMBROGIO: But don't you think that by entrusting the responsibility for the maintenance of children to the community you will provoke such an increase in population that there will no longer be enough for everyone to live on. But of course, you won't want to hear any talk of Malthusianism and will say that it is an absurdity.

GIORGIO: I told you on another occasion that it is absurd to pretend that the present poverty depends on overpopulation and absurd to wish to propose remedies based on Malthusian practices. But I am very willing to recognise the seriousness of the population question, and I admit that in the future, when every new born child is assured of support, poverty could be reborn due to a real excess of population. Emancipated and educated men, when they think it necessary, will consider placing a limit to the overly rapid multiplication of the species; but I would add that they will think seriously about it only when hoarding and privileges, obstacles placed upon production by the greediness of the proprietors and all the social causes of poverty are eliminated, only then will the necessity of achieving a balance between the number of living beings, production capacities, and available space, appear to everyone clear and simple

AMBROGIO: And if people don't want to think about it?

GIORGIO: Well then, all the worse for them!

You don't want to understand: there is no providence, whether divine or natural, that looks after the well-being of humanity. People have to procure their own well being, doing what they think is useful and necessary to reach this goal.

You always say: but what if they don't want to? In this case they will achieve nothing and will always remain at the mercy of the blind forces that surround them.

So it is today: people don't know what to do to become free, or if they know, don't want to do what needs to be done to liberate themselves. And thus, they remain slaves.

But we hope that sooner than you might think they will know what to do and be capable of doing it.

Then they will be free.

ELEVEN

AMBROGIO: The other day you concluded that everything depends on the will. You were saying that if people want to be free, if they want to do what needs to be done to live in a society of equals, everything will be fine: or if not so much the worse for them. This would be all right if they all want the same thing; but if some want to live in anarchy and others prefer the guardianship of a government, if some are prepared to take into consideration the needs of the community and others want to enjoy the benefits derived from social life, but do not want to adapt themselves to the necessities involved, and want to do what they like without taking into account the damage it could do to others, what happens if there is no government that determines and imposes social duties?

GIORGIO: If there is a government, the will of the rulers and of their party and associated interests will triumph – and the problem, which is how to satisfy the will of all, is not resolved. On the contrary, the difficulty is aggravated. The governing fraction can not only use its own resources to ignore or violate the will of others, but has at its disposal the strength of the whole society to impose its will. This is the case in our present society where the working class provides the government with the soldiers and the wealth to keep the workers slaves.

I think I have already told you: we want a society in which everyone has the means to live as they like, where no one can force others to work for them, where no one can compel another to submit to their will. Once two principles are put into practice, liberty for all and the instruments of production for all, everything else will follow naturally, through force of circumstances, and the new society will organise itself in the way that agrees best with the interests of all.

AMBROGIO: And if some want to impose themselves by crude force?

GIORGIO: Then they will be the government; or the candidates for government, and we will oppose them with force. You must understand that if today we want to make a revolution against the government, it is not in order to submit ourselves supinely to new oppressors. If such as these win, the revolution would be defeated, and it would have to be remade.

AMBROGIO: But, you would surely allow some ethical principles, superior to the wills and caprices of humanity, and to which everyone is obliged to conform... at least morally?

GIORGIO: What is this morality that is superior to the will of men? Who prescribed it? From whence does it derive?

Morals change according to the times, the countries, the classes, the circumstances. They express what people at given moments and in given circumstances, regard as the best conduct. In short, for each person good morals accord with what they like or what pleases them, for material or for emotional reasons.

For you morality enjoins respect for the law, that is, submission to the privileges enjoyed by your class; for us it demands a revolt against oppression and the search for the well being of everyone. For us all moral prescriptions are comprehended by love between people.

AMBROGIO: And the criminals? Will you respect their liberty?

GIORGIO: We believe that to act criminally means to violate the liberty of others. When the criminals are many and powerful and have organised their dominance on a stable basis, as is the case, today, with the owners and rulers, there needs to be a revolution to liberate oneself.

When, on the contrary, criminality is reduced to individual

cases of unsuitable behaviour or of illness, we will attempt to find the causes and to introduce them to appropriate remedies.

AMBROGIO: In the meantime? You will need a police force, a magistrature, a penal code, some gaolers, etc...

GIORGIO: And therefore, you would say, the reconstitution of a government, the return to the state of oppression under which we live today.

In fact, the major damage caused by crime is not so much the single and transitory instance of the violation of the rights of a few individuals, but the danger that it will serve as an opportunity and pretext for the constitution of an authority that, with the outward appearance of defending society will subdue and oppress it.

We already know the purpose of the police and the magistrature, and how they are the cause rather than the remedy of innumerable crimes.

We need therefore to try to destroy crime by eliminating the causes; and when there remains a residue of criminals, the collective directly concerned should think of placing them in a position where they can do no harm, without delegating to anyone the specific function of persecuting criminals.

You do know the story of the horse which asked protection from a man, and allowed him to mount on its back?

AMBROGIO: All right. At this point I am only seeking some information and not a discussion.

Another thing. Seeing that in your society all are socially equal, all have a right to the same access to education and development, all have full liberty to choose their own life, how are you going to provide for the necessary tasks. There are pleasant and laborious jobs, healthy and unhealthy jobs. Naturally each person will choose the better jobs – who would do the others, that are often the most necessary?

And then there is the great division between intellectual and manual labour. Don't you think that everyone would like to be doctors, *litterati*, poets, and that no one would wish to cultivate the land, make shoes etc. etc. Well?

GIORGIO: You want to look forward to a future society, a society of equality, liberty and above all solidarity and free agreement, presuming the continuation of the moral and material conditions of today. Naturally the thing appears and is impossible.

When everybody has the means, everyone will reach the maximum material and intellectual development that their natural faculties will permit: everybody will be initiated into intellectual joys and into productive labour; the body and brain will develop harmoniously; at different levels, according to capacity and inclination, everybody will be scientists and *litterati* versed in literature and everybody will be workers.

What would happen then?

Imagine that a few thousand doctors, engineers, *litterati*, and artists, were to be transported to a vast and fertile island, provided with the instruments of work and left to themselves.

Do you think that they will let themselves die of hunger rather than working with their own hands, or that they would kill themselves rather than coming to an agreement and dividing work according to their inclinations and their capacities? If there were jobs that no one wanted to do, they would all do them in turn, and everyone would search for the means to make unhealthy and unpleasant jobs safe and enjoyable.

AMBROGIO: Enough, enough, I must have another thousand questions to put to you, but you wander in a total utopia and find imaginary ways to resolve all the problems.

I would prefer that you talk to me about the ways and means by which you propose to realise your dreams.

GIORGIO: With pleasure, so much so since as far as I am concerned, even though the ideal is useful and necessary as a way of indicating the final goal, the most urgent question is what must be done today and in the immediate future.

We will talk about it next time.

TWELVE

AMBROGIO: So tonight you will talk to us about the means by which you propose to attain your ideals... to create anarchism.

I can already imagine. There will be bombs, massacres, summary executions; and then plunder, arson and similar niceties.

GIORGIO: You, my dear, sir, have simply come to the wrong person – you must have thought you were talking to some official or other who commands European soldiers, when they go *to civilise* Africa or Asia, or when they *civilise* each other back home.

That's not my style, please believe me.

CESARE: I think, my dear sir, that our friend, who has at last shown that he is a reasonable young man although too much of a dreamer, awaits the triumph of ideas through the natural evolution of society, the spread of education, the progress of science, the development of production.

And after all there is nothing wrong with that. If anarchism has to come, it will come, and it is useless to rack our brains to avoid the inevitable.

But then ... it is so far away! Let's live in peace.

GIORGIO: Indeed, would that not be a good reason for you to indulge yourself!

But no, Signor Cesare, I don't rely on evolution, on science and the rest. One would have to wait too long! And, what is worse, one would wait in vain!

Human evolution moves in the direction in which it is driven by the will of humanity, and there is no natural law that says evolution must inevitably give priority to liberty rather than the permanent division of society into two castes, I could almost say into two races, that of the dominators and that of the dominated.

Every state of society, because it has found sufficient reasons to exist, can also persist indefinitely, so long as the dominators don't meet a conscious, active, aggressive opposition from the dominated. The factors of disintegration and spontaneous death which exist in every regime, even when there are compensatory factors of reconstruction and vitality to act as antidotes, can always be neutralized by the skill of whoever disposes of the force of society and directs it as they wish.

I could demonstrate to you, if I wasn't afraid of taking too much time, how the bourgeoisie are protecting themselves from those *natural* tendencies, from which certain socialists were expecting their imminent death.

Science is a potent weapon that can be used equally for good or for evil. And since in the current conditions of inequality, it is more accessible to the privileged than the oppressed, it is more useful to the former than the latter.

Education, at least that which goes beyond a superficial smattering, is almost useless, and is inaccessible to the underprivileged masses – and even then it can be directed in a way chosen by the educators, or rather by those who pay and choose the educators.

AMBROGIO: But, then all that is left is violence!

GIORGIO: Namely, the revolution.

AMBROGIO: Violent revolution? Armed revolution?

GIORGIO: Precisely.

AMBROGIO: Therefore, bombs ...

GIORGIO: Never mind all that, Signor Ambrogio. You are a magistrate, but I don't like having to repeat that this is not a tribunal, and, for the moment at least, I am not a defendant, from whose mouth it would be in your interest to draw some imprudent remark.

The revolution will be violent because you, the dominant class, maintain yourselves with violence and don't show any inclination to give up peacefully. So there will be gunfire, bombs, radio waves that will explode your deposits of explosives and the cartridges in the cartridge-boxes of your soldiers from a distance... all this may happen. These are technical questions that, if you like, we'll leave to the technicians.

What I can assure you of is that, as far as it depends on us, the violence, which has been imposed on us by your violence, will not go beyond the narrow limits indicated by the necessity of the struggle, that is to say that it will above all be determined by the resistance you offer. If the worst should happen, it will be due to your obstinacy and the bloodthirsty education that, by your example, you are providing to the public.

CESARE: But how will you make this revolution, if there are so few of you?

GIORGIO: It is possible that there is only a limited number of us. It suits you to hope so, and I don't want to take this sweet illusion from you. It means that we will be forced to double and then redouble our numbers...

Certainly our task, when there are no opportunities to do more, is to use propaganda to gather a minority of conscious individuals who will know what they have to do and are committed to doing it. Our task is that of preparing the masses, or as much of the masses as possible, to act in the right direction when the occasion arises. And by the right direction we mean: expropriate the current holders of social wealth, throw down the authorities, prevent the formation of new privileges and new forms of government and reorganise directly, through the activity of the workers, production, distribution and the whole of social life.

CESARE: And if the occasion doesn't arise?

GIORGIO: Well, we'll look for ways to make it happen.

PROSPERO: How many illusions you have, my boy!!!

You think that we are still in the time of stone-age weapons.

With modern arms and tactics you would be massacred before you could move.

GIORGIO: Not necessarily. To new arms and tactics it is possible to oppose appropriate responses.

And then again, these arms are actually in the hands of the sons of the people, and you, by forcing everyone to undertake military service, are teaching everybody how to handle them.

Oh! You cannot imagine how really helpless you'll be on the day a sufficient number rebel.

It is we, the proletariat, the oppressed class, who are the electricians and gas-fitters, we who drive the locomotives, it is we who make the explosives and shape the mines, it is we who drive automobiles and aeroplanes, it is we who are the soldiers…it is we, unfortunately, that defend you against ourselves. You only survive because of the unwitting agreement of your victims. Be careful of awakening their consciousness…

And then you know, among anarchists everybody governs their own actions, and your police force is used to looking everywhere, except where the real danger is.

But I do not intend to give you a course in insurrectional technique. This is a matter that...does not concern you.

Good evening.

THIRTEEN

VINCENZO [*Young Republican*]: Permit me to enter into your conversation so that I can ask a few questions and make a few observations?...Our friend Giorgio talks of anarchism, but says that anarchism must come freely, without imposition, through the will of the people. And he also says that to give a free outlet to the people's will there is a need to demolish by insurrection the monarchic and militarist regime which today suffocates and falsifies this will. This is what the republicans want, at least the revolutionary republicans, in other words those who truly want to make the republic. Why then don't you declare yourself a republican?

In a republic the people are sovereign, and if one does what the people want, and they want anarchism there will be anarchism.

GIORGIO: Truly I believe I have always spoken of the *will of humanity* and not the *will of the people*, and if I said the latter it was a form of words, an inexact use of language, that the whole of my conversation serves, after all, to correct.

VINCENZO: But, what is all this concern with words?!! Isn't the public made up of human beings?

GIORGIO: It is not a question of words. It is a question of substance: it is all the difference between *democracy*, which means the government of the people, and *anarchism*, which does not mean government, but liberty for each and everyone.

The people are certainly made up of humanity, that is of a conscious unity, interdependent as far as they choose, but each person has their own sensitivities and their own interests, passions, particular wills, that, according to the situation, augment or annul each other, reinforce or neutralise each other in turn. The strongest, the best-armed will, of an individual, of a party, of a class able to dominate, imposes itself and succeeds in passing itself off as the will of all; in reality that which calls itself the *will of the people* is the will of those who dominate – or it's a hybrid product of numerical calculations which don't exactly correspond to the will of anyone and which satisfies no-one.

Already by their own statements the democrats, that is the republicans (because they are the only true democrats) admit that the so-called government of the people is only the government of the majority, which expresses and carries out its will by means of its representatives. Therefore the "sover-

eigny" of the minority is simply a nominal right that does not translate into action; and note that this "minority" in addition to being often the most advanced and progressive part of the population, may also be the numerical majority when a minority united by a community of interests or ideas, or by their submission to a leader, find themselves facing many discordant factions.

But the party whose candidates succeed and which therefore governs in the name of the majority, is it really a government that expresses the will of the majority? The functioning of a parliamentary system (necessary in every republic that is not a small and isolated independent commune) ensures that each representative is a single unit of the electoral body, one among many, and only counts for a hundredth or a thousandth in the making of laws, which ought in the final analysis be the expression of the will of the majority of electors.

And now, let's leave aside the question of whether the republican regime can carry out the will of all and tell me at least what you want, what would you wish this republic to do, what social institutions ought it to bring into being.

VINCENZO: But it's obvious.

What I want, what all true republicans want is social justice, the emancipation of the workers, equality, liberty and fraternity.

A VOICE: Like they already have in France, in Switzerland and in America.

VINCENZO: Those are not true republics. You should direct your criticism at the true republic that we seek, and not at the various governments, bourgeois, military and clerical that in different parts of the world claim the name of republic. Otherwise in opposing socialism and anarchism I could cite so-called anarchists that are something else altogether.

GIORGIO: Well said. But why on earth haven't the existing republics turned out to be true republics? Why, as a matter of fact, is it that all, or almost all, having started with the ideals of equality, liberty and fraternity which are your ideals and I would say ours also, have been systems of privilege that are becoming entrenched, in which workers are exploited in the extreme, the capitalists are very powerful, the people greatly oppressed and the government as wholly dishonest as in any monarchic regime?

The political institutions, the regulating organs of society, the individual and collective rights recognised by the constitution are the same as they will be in your republic.

Why have the consequences been so bad or at least so negative, and why should they be different when it is your republic.

VINCENZO: Because...because...

GIORGIO: I'll tell you why, and it is that in those republics the economic conditions of the people remained substantially the same; the division of society into a propertied class and a proletarian class remained unaltered, and so true dominion remained in the hands of those who, possessing the monopoly of the means of production, held in their power the great mass of the under-privileged. Naturally the privileged class did its utmost to consolidate its position, which would have been shaken by the revolutionary fervour out of which the republic was born, and soon things returned to what they were before...except, possibly, with respect to those differences, those advances which do not depend on the form of government, but on the growth in the conscious-ness of the workers, on the growth in confidence in its own strength, that the masses acquire every time they succeed in bringing down a government.

VINCENZO: But we completely recognise the importance of the economic question. We will establish a progressive tax that will make the rich shoulder the major share of pub-lic expenses, we will abolish protective duties, we will place a tax on uncultivated lands, we will establish a minimum salary, a ceiling on prices, we will make laws that will pro-tect the workers...

GIORGIO: Even if you succeed in doing all this capitalists will once again find a way to render it useless or turn it to their advantage.

VINCENZO: In that case we will of course expropriate them perhaps without compensation and create communism.

Are you content?

GIORGIO: No, no...communism made through the will of a government instead of through the direct and voluntary work of groups of workers does not really appeal to me. If it was possible, it would be the most suffocating tyranny to which human society has ever been subjected.

But you say: we will do this or that as if because of the fact that you are republicans on the eve of the republic, when the republic is proclaimed you will be the government.

Since the republic is a system of what you call popular sovereignty, and this sovereignty expresses itself by means of universal suffrage, the republican government will be composed of men designated by the popular vote.

And since you have not in the act of republican revolution broken the power of the capitalists by expropriating them in a revolutionary manner, the first republican parliament will be one suited to the capitalists...and if not the first, which may still feel the effects to an extent of the revolutionary storm, certainly successive parliaments will be what the capitalists desire and will be obliged to destroy whatever good the revolution had by chance been able to do.

VINCENZO: But in that case, since anarchism is not possible today, must we calmly support the monarchy for who knows how long?

GIORGIO: By no means. You can count on our cooperation, just as we will be asking for yours, provided that the circumstances become favourable to an insurrectionary movement. Naturally the range of contributions that we will strive to give to that movement will be much broader than yours, but this does not invalidate the common interest we have in the shaking off the yoke that today oppresses both of us. Afterwards we will see.

In the meantime let us spread propaganda together and try to prepare the masses so that the next revolutionary movement sets in train the most profound social transformation possible, and leaves open, broadly and easily, the road toward further progress.

FOURTEEN

CESARE: Let's resume our usual conversation.

Apparently, the thing that most immediately interests you is the insurrection; and I admit that, however difficult it seems, it could be staged and won, sooner or later. In essence governments rely on soldiers; and the conscripted soldiers, who are forced reluctantly into the army barracks, are an unreliable weapon. Faced with a general uprising of the people, the soldiers who are themselves of the people, won't hold on for long; and as soon as the charm and the fear of discipline is broken, they will either disband or join the people.

I admit therefore that by spreading a lot of propaganda among the workers and the soldiers, or among the youth who tomorrow will be soldiers, you put yourselves in a position to take advantage of a favourable situation – economic crises, unsuccessful war, general strike, famine etc. etc. – to bring down the government.

But then?

You will tell me: the people themselves will decide, organise, etc. But these are words. What will probably take place is that after a shorter or longer period of disorder, of dissipation and probably of massacres, a new government will take the place of the other, will re-establish order...and everything will continue as before.

To what purpose then was such a waste of energy?

GIORGIO: If it should occur as you suggest, it does not mean that the insurrection would have been useless. After a revolution things do not return to as they were before because the people have enjoyed a period of liberty and have tested their own strength, and it is not easy to make them accept once again the previous conditions. The new government, if government there has to be, will feel that it cannot remain safely in power unless it gives some satisfaction, and normally it tries to justify its rise to power by giving itself the title of interpreter and successor of the revolution.

Naturally the real task the government will set itself will be to prevent the revolution going any further and to restrict and to alter, with the aim of domination, the gains of the revolution; but it could not return things to how they were before.

This is what has happened in all past revolutions.

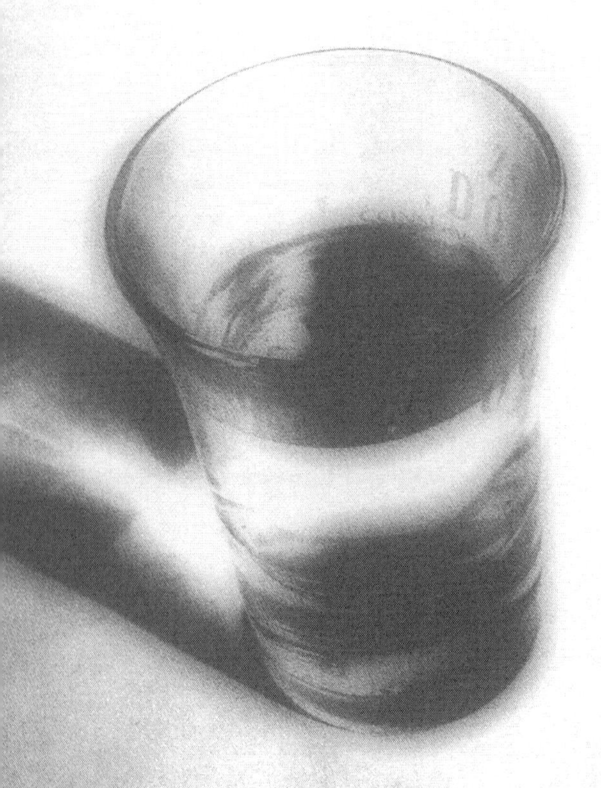

However we have reason to hope that in the next revolution we will do a lot better.

CESARE: Why?

GIORGIO: Because in past revolutions all the revolutionaries, all the initiators and principal actors of the revolution wanted to transform society by means of laws and wanted a government that would make and impose those laws. It was inevitable therefore that it would produce a new government – and it was natural that a new government thought first of all of *governing*, that is of consolidating its power and, in order to do this, of forming around itself a party and a privileged class with a common interest in it remaining permanently in power.

But now a new factor has appeared in history, which is represented by anarchists. Now there are revolutionaries who want to make a revolution with distinctly anti-government aims, therefore the establishment of a new government would face an obstacle that has never been found in the past.

Furthermore, past revolutionaries, wanting to make the social transformation they desired by means of laws, addressed the masses solely for the basic cooperation they could provide, and did not bother to give them a consciousness of what could be wished for and of the way in which they could fulfil their aspirations. So, naturally, the people, liable to self-destruction, themselves asked for a government, when there was a need to reorganise everyday social life.

On the other hand, with our propaganda and with workers' organisations we aim to form a conscious minority that knows what it wants to do, and which, intermingled with the masses, could provide for the immediate necessities and take those initiatives, which on other occasions were waited for from the government.

CESARE: Very well; but since you will only be a minority, and probably in many parts of the country you will not have any influence, a government will be established just the same and you will have to endure it.

GIORGIO: It is more than likely that a government will succeed in establishing itself; but whether we'll have to put up with it...that we will see.

Note this well. In past revolutions there was a primary concern to create a new government and the orders were awaited from this government. And in the meantime things remained substantially the same, or rather the economic conditions of the masses deteriorated because of the interruption of industry and commerce. Therefore people quickly became tired of it all; there was a hurry to get it over and done with and hostility from the public towards those who wanted to prolong the state of insurrection for too long. And so whoever demonstrated a capacity to restore order, whether it be a soldier of fortune, or a shrewd and daring politician, or possibly the same sovereign who had been thrown out, would be welcomed with popular applause as a peacemaker and a liberator.

We on the contrary understand revolution very differently. We want the social transformation at which the revolution aims to begin to be realised from the first insurrectional act. We want the people immediately to take possession of existing wealth; declare gentlemen's mansions public domain, and provide through voluntary and active initiatives minimal housing for all the population, and at once put in hand through the work of the constructor's association, the construction of as many new houses as is considered necessary. We want to make all the available food products community property and organise, always through voluntary operations and under the true control of the public, an equal distribution for all. We want the agricultural workers to take possession of uncultivated land and that of the landowners and by so doing convince the latter that now the land belongs to the labourers. We want workers to remove themselves from the direction of the owners and continue production on their own account and for the public. We would like to establish at once exchange relationships among the diverse productive associations and the different communes; – and at the same time we want to burn, to destroy, all the titles and all material signs of individual property and state domination. In short, we want from the first moment to make the masses feel the benefits of the revolution and so disturb things that it will be impossible to re-establish the ancient order.

CESARE: And do you think that all of this is easy to carry out?

GIORGIO: No, I'm well aware of all the difficulties that we will be confronting; I clearly foresee that our programme cannot be applied everywhere at once, and that where applied it will give rise to a thousand disagreements and a thousand errors. But the single fact that there are people who want to apply it and will try and to apply it wherever possible, is already a guarantee that at this point the revolution can no longer be a simple political transformation and must put in train a profound change in the whole of social life.

Moreover, the bourgeoisie did something similar in the great French Revolution at the end of the 18th century, although to a smaller degree, and the ancien régime could not re-establish itself notwithstanding the Empire and the Restoration.

CESARE: But if, despite all your good or bad intentions, a government establishes itself, all your projects will go up in the air, and you would have to submit to the law like everybody else.

GIORGIO: And why is that?

That a government or governments will establish itself is certainly very probable. There are a lot of people that like to command and a lot more that are disposed to obey!

But it is very difficult to see how this government could impose itself, make itself accepted and become a regular government, if there are enough revolutionaries in the country, and they have learned enough to involve the masses in preventing a new government finding a way to become strong and stable.

A government needs soldiers, and we will do everything possible to deny them soldiers; a government needs money and we will do all we can to ensure that no one pays taxes and no one gives it credit.

There are some municipalities and perhaps some regions in Italy where revolutionaries are fairly numerous and the workers quite prepared to proclaim themselves autonomous and look after their own affairs, refusing to recognise the government and to receive its agents or to send representatives to it.

These regions, these municipalities will be centres of revolutionary influence, against which any government will be impotent, if we act quickly and do not give it time to arm and consolidate itself.

CESARE: But this is civil war!

GIORGIO: It may very well be. We are for peace, we yearn for peace... but we will not sacrifice the revolution to our desire of peace. We will not sacrifice it because only by this route can we reach a true and permanent peace.

FIFTEEN

GINO [*Worker*]: I have heard that you discuss social questions in the evenings and I have come to ask, with the permission of these gentlemen, a question of my friend Giorgio.

Tell me, is it true that you anarchists want to remove the police force.

GIORGIO: Certainly. What! Don't you agree? Since when have you become a friend of police and *carabinieri*?

GINO: I am not their friend, and you know it. But I'm also not the friend of murderers and thieves and I would like my goods and my life to be guarded and guarded well.

GIORGIO: And who guards you from the guardians?...

Do you think that men become thieves and murderers without a reason?

Do you think that the best way to provide for one's own security is by offering up one's neck to a gang of people who, with the excuse of defending us, oppress us and practice extortion, and do a thousand times more damage than all the thieves and all the murderers? Wouldn't it be better to destroy the causes of evil, doing it in such a way that everybody could live well, without taking bread from the mouths of others, and doing it in a way so that everyone could educate and develop themselves and banish from their hearts the evil passions of jealousy, hatred and revenge?

GINO: Come off it! Human beings are bad by nature, and if there weren't laws, judges, soldiers and *carabinieri* to hold us in check, we would devour each other like wolves.

GIORGIO: If this was the case, it would be one more reason for not giving anybody the power to command and to dispose of the liberty of others. Forced to fight against everybody, each person with average strength, would run the same risk in the struggle and could alternatively be a winner and a loser: we would be savages, but at least we could enjoy the relative liberty of the jungle and the fierce emotions of the beasts of prey. But if voluntarily we should give to a few the right and the power to impose their will, then since, according to you, the simple fact of being human predisposes us to devour one another, it will be the same as voting ourselves into slavery and poverty.

You are deceiving yourself however, my dear friend. Humanity is good or bad according to circumstances. What

is common in human beings is the instinct for self-preservation, and an aspiration for well-being and for the full development of one's own powers. If in order to live well you
need to treat others harshly, only a few will have the strength
necessary to resist the temptation. But put human beings in
a society of their fellow creatures with conditions conducive
to well-being and development, and it will need a great
effort to be bad, just as today it needs great effort to be
good.

GINO: All right, it may be as you say. But in the meantime
while waiting for social transformation the police prevent
crimes from being committed.

GIORGIO: Prevent?!

GINO: Well then, they prevent a great number of crimes,
and bring to justice the perpetrators of those offences which
they were not able to prevent.

GIORGIO: Not even this is true. The influence of the police
on the number and the significance of crimes is almost nothing. In fact, however much the organisation of the magistrature, of the police and the prisons is reformed, or the number of policemen decreased or increased, while the economic and moral conditions of the people remain unchanged,
delinquency will remain more or less constant.

On the other hand, it only needs the smallest modification in
the relations between proprietors and workers, or a change
in the price of wheat and other vitally necessary foods, or a
crisis that leaves workers without work, or the spreading of

our ideas which opens new horizons for people making them smile with new hope, and immediately the effect on the increase or decrease in the number of crimes will be noted.

The police, it is true, send delinquents to prison, when they can catch them; but this, since it does not prevent new offences, is an evil added to an evil, a further unnecessary suffering inflicted on human beings.

And even if the work of the police force succeeds in putting off a few offences, that would not be sufficient, by a long way, to compensate for the offences it provokes, and the harassment to which it subjects the public.

The very function they carry out makes the police suspicious of, and puts them in conflict with, the whole of the public; it makes them hunters of humanity; it leads them to become ambitious to discover some "great" cases of delinquency, and it creates in them a special mentality that very often leads them to develop some distinctly antisocial instincts. It is not rare to find that a police officer, who should prevent or discover crime, instead provokes it or invents it, to promote their career or simply to make themselves important and necessary.

GINO: But, then the policemen themselves would be the same as criminals! Such things occur occasionally, the more so that police personnel are not always recruited from the best part of the population, but in general...

GIORGIO: Generally the background environment has an inexorable effect, and professional distortion strikes even those who call for improvement.

Tell me: what can be, or what can become of the morals of those who are obligated by their salaries, to persecute, to arrest, to torment anyone pointed out to them by their superiors, without worrying whether the person is guilty or innocent, a criminal or an angel?

GINO: Yes...but...

GIORGIO: Let me say a few words about the most important part of the question; in other words, about the so called offences that the police undertake to restrain or prevent.

Certainly among the acts that the law punishes there are those that are and always will be bad actions; but there are exceptions which result from the state of brutishness and desperation to which poverty reduces people.

Generally however the acts that are punished are those which offend against the privileges of the upper-class and those that attack the government in the exercise of its authority. It is in this manner that the police, effectively or not, serve to protect, not society as a whole, but the upper-class, and to keep the people submissive.

You were talking of thieves. Who is more of a thief than the owners who get wealthy stealing the produce of the workers' labour?

You were talking about murderers. Who is more of a murderer than capitalists who, by not renouncing the privilege of being in command and living without working, are the cause of dreadful privations and the premature death of millions of workers, let alone a continuing slaughter of children?

These thieves and murderers, far more guilty and far more dangerous than those poor people who are pushed toward crime by the miserable conditions in which they find themselves, are not a concern of the police: quite the contrary!...

GINO: In short, you think that once having made the revolution, humanity will become, out of the blue, so many little angels. Everybody will respect the rights of others; everybody will wish the best for one another and help each other; there will be no more hatreds, nor jealousies...an earthly paradise, what nonsense?!

GIORGIO: Not at all. I don't believe that moral transformation will come suddenly, out of the blue. Of course, a large, an immense change will take place through the simple fact that bread is assured and liberty gained; but all the bad passions, which have become embodied in us through the age-old influence of slavery and of the struggle between people, will not disappear at a stroke. There will still be for a long time those who will feel tempted to impose their will on others with violence, who will wish to exploit favourable circumstances to create privileges for themselves, who will retain an aversion for work inspired by the conditions of slavery in which today they are forced to labour, and so on.

GINO: So even after the revolution we will have to defend ourselves against criminals?

GIORGIO: Very likely. Provided that those who are then considered criminals are not those who rebel rather than dying of hunger, and still less those who attack the existing organisation of society and seek to replace it with a better one; but those who would cause harm to everyone, those who would encroach on personal integrity, liberty and the well being of others.

GINO: All right, so you will always need a police force.

GIORGIO: But not at all. It would truly be a great piece of foolishness to protect oneself from a few violent people, a few idlers and some degenerates, by opening a school for idleness and violence and forming a body of cut-throats, who will get used to considering citizens as jail bait and who will make hunting people their principal and only occupation.

GINO: What, then!

GIORGIO: Well, we will defend ourselves.

GINO: And do you think that is possible?

GIORGIO: Not only do I think it is possible that the people will defend themselves without delegating to anyone the special function of the defence of society, but I am sure it is the only effective method.

Tell me! If tomorrow someone who is sought after by the police comes to you, will you denounce him?

GINO: What, are you mad? Not even if they were the worst of all murderers. What do you take me for a police officer?!

GIORGIO: Ah! Ah! The police officers' occupation must be a terrible one, if anyone with self-respect thinks themselves dishonoured by taking it on, even when they think it to be useful and necessary to society.

And now, tell me something else. If you happened upon a sick person with an infectious disease or a dangerous madman would you take them to hospital?

GINO: Certainly.

GIORGIO: Even by force?

GINO: But...You must understand! Leaving them free could harm a lot of people!

GIORGIO: Now explain to me, why do you take great care not to denounce a murderer, while you would take a madman or a plague-stricken person to hospital, if necessary by force?

GINO: Well...first of all I find being a policeman repugnant, while I consider it a honourable and humanitarian thing to care for the sick.

GIORGIO: Well you can already see that the first effect of the police is to make the citizens wash their hands of social defence, and actually place them on the side of those who rightly or wrongly the police persecute.

GINO: It is also that when I take someone to hospital I know that I am leaving them in the hands of the doctors, who try to cure them, so that they can be at liberty as soon as they no longer are a threat to other people. In every case, even if incurable, they will try to alleviate suffering and will never inflict a more severe treatment than is strictly necessary. If doctors did not do their duties, the public would make them do so, because it is well understood that people are kept in hospital to be cured and not to be tormented.

While on the contrary, if one delivers someone into the hands of the police, they seek from ambition to try to condemn them, little caring whether they are guilty or innocent; then they put them in prison, where, instead of seeking their improvement through loving care, they do everything to make them suffer, make them more embittered, then release them as an even more dangerous enemy to society than they were before they went to prison.

But, this could be changed through a radical reform.

GIORGIO: In order to reform, my dear fellow, or to destroy an institution, the first thing is not to establish a corporation interested in preserving it.

The police (and what I say of the police applies also to the magistrates) in carrying out their profession of sending people to prison and beating them up when there is an opportunity, will always end up considering themselves as being opposed to the public. They furiously pursue the true or assumed delinquent with the same passion with which a hunter pursues game, but at the same time it is in the interests of the police that there are more delinquents because they are the reason for their existence, and the greater the number and the harmfulness of delinquents grow, so does the power and the social importance of the police!

In order for crime to be treated rationally, in order to seek for its causes and really do everything possible to eliminate it, it is necessary for this task to be entrusted to those who are exposed to and suffer the consequences of crime, in other words the whole public, and not those to whom the existence of crime is a source of power and earnings.

GINO: Oh! It could be you are right. Until next time.

SIXTEEN

PIPPO [*War cripple*]: I've had enough! Please allow me to tell you that I am amazed, I would almost say indignant that, even though you possess the most diverse opinions, you seem to agree in ignoring the essential question, that of the fatherland, that of securing the greatness and the glory of our Italy.

Prospero, Cesare, Vincenzo, *and everyone present, other than* Giorgio and Luigi (a young socialist), *uproariously protest their love for Italy and* Ambrogio *says on everyone's behalf.* In these discussions we have not talked of Italy, as we have not talked of our mothers. It wasn't necessary to talk about what was already understood, of what is superior to any opinion, to any discussion. Please Pippo do not doubt our patriotism, not even that of Giorgio.

GIORGIO: But, no; my patriotism can certainly be doubted, because I am not a patriot.

PIPPO: I already guessed that: you are one of those that shouts *down with Italy* and would like to see our country humiliated, defeated, dominated by foreigners.

GIORGIO: But not at all. These are the usual slanders with which our opponents try to deceive the people in order to prejudice them against us. I don't rule out there being people who in good faith believe this humbug, but this is the result of ignorance and a lack of understanding.

We don't want of domination of any kind and therefore we could not want Italy to be dominated by other countries, just like we don't want Italy to dominate others.

We consider the whole world as our homeland, all humanity as our brothers and sisters; therefore, for us, it would simply be absurd to wish to damage and humiliate the country in which we live; in which we have our dear ones, whose language we speak best, the country that gives us the most and to which we give the most in terms of the exchange of work, ideas and affection.

AMBROGIO: But this country is the fatherland, that you continually curse.

GIORGIO: We don't curse our fatherland, or anybody else's country. We curse patriotism, that which you call patriotism, which is national arrogance, that is the preaching of hatred towards other countries, a pretext for pitting people against people in deadly wars, in order to serve sinister capitalist interests and the immoderate ambitions of sovereigns and petty politicians.

VINCENZO: Easy, easy.

You are right if you talk of the *patriotism* of a great many capitalists and a great many monarchists for whom the love of the country is really a pretext: and, like yourself, I despise and loathe those who don't risk anything for the country and in the name of the fatherland enrich themselves on the sweat and the blood of workers and honest folk from all classes. But there are people who are really patriots, who have sacrificed and are ready to sacrifice everything, their possessions, liberty and their life for their country.

You know that republicans have always been fired by the highest patriotism, and that have always met their responsibilities squarely.

GIORGIO: I always admire those who sacrifice themselves for their ideas, but this does not stop me seeing that the ideals of the republicans and the sincere patriots, who are certainly found in all parties, have at this point become out-of-date and only serve to give to governments and capitalists a way of masking their real aims with ideals and swaying the unconscious masses and the enthusiastic youth.

VINCENZO: What do you mean, out-of-date?! The love of one's country is a natural sentiment of the human heart and will never become out-of-date.

GIORGIO: That which you call love of one's country is the attachment to that country to which you have strongest moral ties and that provides the greatest certainty of material well being; and it is certainly natural and will always remain so, at least until civilization has progressed to the point where every person will *de facto* find their country in any part of the world. But this has nothing in common with the myth of the "fatherland" which makes you consider other people as inferior, which makes you desire the domination of your country over others, which prevents you from appreciating and using the work of so-called foreigners, and which makes you consider workers as having more in common with their bosses and the police of their country than with workers from other countries, with whom they share the same interests and aspirations.

After all, our international, cosmopolitan feelings are still being developed, as a continuation of the progress already made. You may feel more attached to your native village or to your region for a thousand sentimental and material reasons, but it does not mean that you are parochial or tied to your region: you pride yourself on being Italian and, if the necessity arises, you would place the general interests of Italy above regional or local interests. If you believe that broadening the notion of one's country from commune to nation has been an advance, why stop there and not embrace the entire world in a general love for the human kind and in a fraternal co-operation among all people?

Today the relations between countries, the exchanges of raw materials and of agricultural and industrial products are already such that a country which wished to isolate itself from others, or worse, place itself in conflict with others, would condemn itself to an attenuated existence and com-

plete and utter failure. Already there is an abundance of men who because of their relationships, because of their kind of studies and work, because of their economic position, consider themselves and truly are citizens of the world.

Moreover, can't you see that everything that is great and beautiful in the world is of a global and supranational character. Science is international, so too is art, so too is religion which, in spite of its lies, is a great demonstration of humanity's spiritual activity. As Signor Ambrogio would say, rights and morals are universal, because everyone tries to extend their own conceptions to every human being. Any new truth discovered in whatever part of the world, any new invention, any ingenious product of the human brain is useful, or ought to be useful to the whole of humanity.

To return to isolation, to rivalry and hatred between peoples, to persist in a narrow-minded and misanthropic patriotism, would mean placing oneself outside the great currents of progress which press humanity toward a future of peace and fraternity, it would be to place oneself outside and against civilization.

CESARE: You always speak of peace and fraternity; but let me ask you a practical question. If, for instance, the Germans or the French should come to Milan, Rome or Naples to destroy our artistic monuments, and to kill or oppress our fellow-countrymen, what would you do? Would you be unmoved?

GIORGIO: Whatever are you saying? I would certainly be extremely distressed and would do whatever I could to prevent it. But, note this well, I would be equally distressed and, being able, would do everything to prevent Italians going to destroy, oppress and kill in Paris, Vienna, Berlin... or in Libya.

CESARE: Really *equally* distressed?

GIORGIO: Perhaps not in practice. I would feel worse for the wrong-doings done in Italy because it's in Italy I have more friends, I know Italy better, and so my feelings would be deeper and more immediate. But this does not mean that the wrongdoings committed in Berlin would be less wrong than those committed in Milan.

It is as if they were to kill a brother, a friend. I would certainly suffer more than I would had they killed someone I did not know: but this does not mean that the killing of someone unknown to me is less criminal than the killing of a friend.

PIPPO: All right. But what did you do to stop a possible invasion of Milan by the Germans?

GIORGIO: I didn't do anything. Actually my friends and I did all we could to keep out of the fray; because we were not able to do what would have been useful and necessary.

PIPPO: What do you mean?

GIORGIO: It's obvious. We found ourselves in a position of having to defend the interests of our bosses, our oppressors, and having to do so by killing some of our brothers, the workers of other countries driven to the slaughterhouse, just as we were, by their bosses and oppressors. And we refused to be used as an instrument of those who are our real enemy, that is our bosses.

If, firstly, we had been able to free ourselves from our internal enemies, then we would have been able to defend our country and not the country of the bosses. We could have offered a fraternal hand to the foreign workers sent against us, and if they had not understood and had wished to continue to serve their masters by opposing us, we would have defended ourselves.

AMBROGIO: You are only concerned with the interests of the workers, with the interests of your class, without understanding that the nation is above class interests. There are some sentiments, some traditions, some interests that unite all the people of the same nation, despite differences in their conditions and all the antagonisms of class.

And then again, there is the pride in one's roots. Aren't you proud of being Italian, of belonging to a country that has given civilization to the world and even today, in spite of everything, is at the forefront of progress?

How is it you do not feel the need to defend Latin civilization against Teutonic barbarity?

GIORGIO: Please, let's not talk about civilization and the barbarism of this or that country.

I could immediately say to you that if the workers are not able to appreciate your "Latin civilization" the fault is yours, the fault of the bourgeoisie that took away from the workers

the means to educate themselves. How can you expect someone to be passionate about something about which you
have kept them ignorant?

But, stop misleading us. Would you have us believe that the
Germans are more barbaric than anyone else, when for
years you yourself were admiring anything coming from
Germany? If tomorrow political conditions change and capitalist interests are oriented differently, you would once again
say that Germans are at the forefront of civilization and that
the French or the English are barbarians.

What does this mean? If one country finds itself more
advanced than another it has the duty to spread its civilization, to help its fellows who are backward and not profit
from its superiority to oppress and exploit... because any
abuse of power leads to corruption and decadence.

AMBROGIO: But, in any case, you do at least respect
national solidarity which must be superior to any class com-
petition.

GIORGIO: I understand. It is this pretence of national solidarity which particularly interests you, and it is this which
what we struggle against in particular. National solidarity
means solidarity between capitalists and workers, between
oppressors and oppressed, in other words acquiescence by
the oppressed to their state of subjection.

The interests of the workers are opposed to those of the
employers, and when in special circumstances they find
themselves temporarily in agreement, we seek to make them
into antagonists, given that human emancipation and all

future progress depend upon the struggle between workers and owners, that must lead to the complete disappearance of exploitation and oppression of one person by another.

You still try to deceive workers with the lies of nationalism: but in vain. The workers have already understood that the workers of all countries are their comrades, and that all capitalists and all governments, domestic or foreign, are their enemies.

And with this I will say good evening. I know that I haven't convinced neither the magistrates nor the proprietors who have listened to me. But, perhaps I haven't spoken in vain for Pippo, Vincenzo and Luigi, who are proletarians like myself.

SEVENTEEN

LUIGI [*a socialist*]: Since everyone here has stated their opinion, allow me to state mine?

These are just some of my own ideas, and I don't want to expose myself to the combined intolerance of the bourgeoisie and the anarchists.

GIORGIO: I am amazed that you speak like that.

Since we are both workers we can, and must, consider ourselves friends and comrades, but you seem to believe that anarchists are the enemies of socialists. On the contrary, we are their friends, their collaborators.

Even if many notable socialists have attempted and still attempt to oppose socialism to anarchism, the truth is that, if socialism means a society or the aspiration for a society in which humans live in fellowship, in which the well being of all is a condition for the well being of each, in which no one is a slave or exploited and each person has the means to develop to the maximum extent possible and to enjoy in peace all the benefits of civilization and of communal work, not only are we socialists, but we have the right to consider ourselves the most radical and consistent socialists.

After all, even Signor Ambrogio, who has sent so many of us to gaol, knows we were the first to introduce, to explain and to propagate socialism; and if little by little we ended up abandoning the name and calling ourselves simply anarchists, it was because there arose alongside us another school, dictatorial and parliamentary, which managed to prevail and to make of socialism such a hybrid and accommodating thing that it was impossible to reconcile with our ideals and our methods a doctrine that was repugnant to our nature

LUIGI: In fact, I have understood your arguments and we certainly agree on many things, especially the criticisms of capitalism.

But we don't agree on everything, firstly because anarchists only believe in revolution and renounce the more civilized means of struggle that have replaced those violent methods which were perhaps necessary once upon a time – and secondly, because even if we should conclude with a violent revolution, it would be necessary to put in power a new government to do things in an orderly manner and not leave everything to arbitrary actions and the fury of the masses.

GIORGIO: Well, let's discuss this further. Do you seriously believe that it is possible radically to transform society, to demolish privileges, throw out the government, expropriate the bourgeoisie without resorting to force?

I hope that you don't delude yourself that owners and rulers will surrender without resistance, without making use of the forces at their disposal, and can somehow be persuaded to play the part of sacrificial victims. Otherwise, ask these gentlemen here who, if they could, would get rid of you and me with great pleasure and with great speed.

LUIGI: No, I don't have any of those illusions.

But since today the workers are the great majority of the electorate and have the right to vote in administrative and political elections, it seems to me that, if they were conscious and willing, they could without too much effort put in power people whom they could trust, socialists and, if you want, even some anarchists, who could make good laws, nationalise the land and workshops and introduce socialism.

GIORGIO: Of course, if the workers were conscious and committed!

But if they were developed enough to be able to understand the causes of their problems and the remedies to them, if they were truly determined to emancipate themselves, then the revolution could be made with little, or no, violence, and the workers themselves could do whatever they wanted and there wouldn't be a need to send to parliament and into government people, who, even if they didn't allow themselves to become intoxicated and corrupted by the allurements of power, as unfortunately happens, find themselves unable to provide for social needs and do what the electors expect of them.

But unfortunately the workers, or the great majority of them, are not conscious or committed; they live in conditions that do not admit of the possibility of emancipating themselves morally unless there is firstly an improvement in their material condition. So, the transformation of society must come about through the initiative and the work of those minority groups who due to fortunate circumstances have been able to elevate themselves above the common level – numerical minorities which end up being the predominant force capable of pulling along with them the backward masses.

Look at the facts, and soon you will see that, precisely because of the moral and material conditions in which the proletariat finds itself, the bourgeoisie and the government always succeed in obtaining from the parliament what suits them. That's why they concede universal suffrage and allow it to function. If they should see any danger of being legally dispossessed they would be the first to depart from legality and violate what they call the popular will. Already they do this on every occasion the laws by mistake work against them.

LUIGI: You say this, but in the meantime we see the number of socialist deputies is always increasing. One day they will be the majority and...

GIORGIO: But, can't you see that when socialists enter parliament, they immediately become tamed and, from being a danger, they become collaborators, and supporters of the prevailing order? After all, by sending socialists to parliament we render a service to the bourgeoisie because the most active, able and popular people are removed from the heart of the masses and transported into a bourgeoisie environment.

Furthermore, as I've already told you, when the socialist members of parliament really become a danger, the government will drive them from parliament at bayonet point and suppress universal suffrage.

LUIGI: It may seem like this to you, because you always see things in terms of a world in extreme crisis.

The reverse is true. The world moves a little at a time by gradual evolution.

It is necessary for the proletariat to prepare to take over from the bourgeoisie, by educating itself, by organising itself, by sending its representatives to the bodies which decide and make laws; and when it becomes mature it will take everything into its own hands, and the new society to which we aspire will be established.

In all civilized countries the number of socialist deputies is increasing and naturally so too is their support among the masses.

Some day they will certainly be the majority, and if then the bourgeoisie and its government will not give in peacefully and attempts violently to suppress the popular will, we will reply to violence with violence.

It is necessary to take time. It is useless and damaging wanting to try to force the laws of nature and of history.

GIORGIO: Dear Luigi, the laws of nature do not need defenders: they produce respect for themselves. People laboriously discover them and make use of their discovery either to do good or evil; but beware of accepting as natural laws the social facts that interested parties (in our case the economists and sociologists who defend the bourgeoisie) describe as such.

As far as the "laws of history", they are formulated after history is made. Let us first of all make history.

The world moves slowly, or quickly, it goes forward or backward, as the result of an indefinite number of natural and human factors, and it is an error to feel confident of a continuous evolution which always moves in the same direction.

At present, it is certainly true that society is in a continuous, slow evolution; but evolution in essence means change, and if some changes are those that lead in the right direction for us, that favour the elevation of humanity towards a superior ideal of community and of liberty, others instead reinforce the existing institutions or drive back and annul the progress already realised.

While people remain in opposition to each other, no gains are secure, no progress in social organisation can be considered definitely won.

We must utilize and encourage all the elements of progress and combat, obstruct and try to neutralise regressive and conservative forces.

Today the fate of humanity depends on the struggle between workers and exploiters and whatever conciliation there is between the two hostile classes, whatever collaboration there is between capitalists and workers, between government and people, carried out with the intention or on the pretext of toning down social disputes, only serves to favour the class of oppressors, to reinforce the tottering institutions and, what is worse still, to separate from the masses the most developed proletarian elements and turn them into a new privileged class with an interest shared with the barons of industry, finance and politics, in maintaining the great majority of the people in a state of inferiority and subjection.

You talk of evolution, and seem to think that necessarily and inevitably, whether people want it or not, humanity will arrive at socialism, in other words a society created for the equal interest of all, in which the means of production belong to all, where everybody will be a worker, where everybody will enjoy with equal rights all the benefits of civilisation.

But this is not true. Socialism will come about if the people want it and do what is necessary to achieve it. Because otherwise it is possible that, instead of socialism, a social situation could eventuate in which the differences between people are greater and more permanent, in which humanity becomes divided into two different races, the gentlefolk and the servants, with an intermediate class which would serve to insure through the combination of intelligence and brute force, the dominance of one over the other – or there could simply be a continuation of the present state of continuous struggle, an alternation of improvements and deteriorations, of crises and periodic wars.

Actually, I would say that if we were to leave things to their natural course, evolution would probably move in the opposite direction to the one we desire, it would move towards the consolidation of privileges, towards a stable equilibrium established in favour of the present rulers, because it is natural that strength belongs to the strong, and who starts the contest with certain advantages over their opponent will always gain more advantages in the course of the struggle.

LUIGI: Perhaps you are right; this is precisely why we need to utilize all the means at our disposal: education, organisation and political struggle...

GIORGIO: All means, yes, but all the means that lead to our goal.

Education, certainly. It is the first thing that is needed, because if we don't act on the minds of individuals, if we don't awaken their consciences, if we don't stimulate their senses, if we don't excite their will, progress will not be possible. And by education I don't so much mean book-learning, although, it too is necessary, but not very accessible to proletarians, rather, the education that one acquires through conscious contact with society, propaganda, discussions, concern with public issues, the participation in the struggles for one's own and others' improvement.

This education of the individual is necessary and would be sufficient to transform the world if it could be extended to all.

But, unfortunately, that is not possible. People are influenced, dominated, one could almost say shaped, by the environment in which they live; and when the environment is not suitable one can progress only by fighting against it. At any given moment there are only a limited number of individuals who are capable, either because of inherited capacities or because of specially favourable circumstances, of elevating themselves above the environment, reacting against it and contributing to its transformation.

This is why it is a conscious minority that must break the ice and violently change the exterior circumstances.

Organisation: A great and necessary thing, provided that it is used to fight the bosses and not to reach an agreement with them.

Political struggle: Obviously, provided by it we mean struggle against the government and not co-operation with the government.

Pay close attention. If you want to improve the capitalist system and make it tolerable, and hence sanction and perpetuate it, then certain accommodations, certain amounts of collaboration may be acceptable; but if you truly want to overthrow the system, then you must clearly place yourself outside and against the system itself.

And since the revolution is necessary and since whichever way you look at it the problem will only be solved through revolution, don't you think we should prepare ourselves from now on, spiritually and materially, instead of deluding the masses and giving them the hope of being able to emancipate themselves without sacrifices and bloody struggles.

LUIGI: That's fine. Let's suppose that you are right and that revolution is inevitable. There are also a lot of socialists who say the same. But it will always be necessary to establish a new government to direct and organise the revolution.

GIORGIO: Why? If among the masses there isn't a sufficient number of revolutionaries, manual and non-manual workers, capable of providing for the needs of the struggle and of life, the revolution will not be made, or if made, will not triumph. And if a sufficient number exist what is a government good for other than to paralyse popular initiative and in substance to choke the very revolution itself.

In fact, what can a parliamentary or a dictatorial government do?

It must first of all think of and insure its own existence as a government, in other words establish an armed force to defend itself against its opponents and to impose its own will on recalcitrants; then it would have to inform itself, study, try to conciliate the wills and the interests in conflict and hence make laws...which most likely will not please anybody.

In the meantime it is necessary to go on living. Either property will have *de facto* passed into the hands of the workers, and then, because it is necessary to provide for everyday necessities, these same workers would have to solve the problems of everyday life without awaiting the decisions of the rulers, the latter thus...can now only declare their own uselessness as rulers and blend in with the crowd as workers.

Or property will have remained in the hands of proprietors, then, they, holding and disposing of wealth as they please, would remain the true arbiters of social life, and would make sure that the new government composed of socialists (not anarchists, because anarchists do not want to govern nor be governed) will either submit to the wishes of the bourgeoisie or be quickly swept away.

I will not dwell on this because I have to go and I don't know when I will be returning. It will be a while before we see each other.

Think about what I have said – I hope that when I will return I will find a new comrade.

Goodbye to you all

More Freedom Press books

A Summer in the Park – A Journal of Speakers' Corner
Tony Allen
£8.50

"Having an audience of easily distracted browsers harbouring hit and run snipers demands a house style of 'dramatic conflict' raw and obvious. A take-no-prisoners gladiatorial confrontation with the speaker as devil's advocate remains the preferred tried and tested format. Even the rough-house of street theatre is subtle by comparison."

Zapata of Mexico
Peter E. Newell
£9.50

Who was Zapata? Man, myth, inspiration or movie icon? Zapata's memory, like his ghost, rides on in Mexico.

William Blake – Visionary Anarchist
Peter Marshall
£4.50

On Blake's complete writings, his poetry and his prose. It offers a lively and perceptive account of his thought, ranging from his philosophy, his critique of existing society and culture, to his vision of a free world. Marshall presents Blake as a forerunner of modern anarchism and social ecology.

About Anarchism
Nicolas Walter
£4.20

This is a new edition of the classic work by Nicolas Walter, who was a writer, journalist and active protester against the power of the state.

Talking Houses

Colin Ward
£6.00

How can so basic a human need as shelter present permanent problems for a significant section of the population? As one of the few inter-
nationally known libertarian writers in the field of housing and other
social issues, and with a keen observation informed by broad personal
experience, Ward is well placed to both diagnose the malady and suggest remedies.

Anarchist Writings of William Godwin

Edited by Peter Marshall
£5.95

William Godwin is the first exponent of anarchism. He is not only the
greatest British radical philosopher, but a pioneer in libertarian education, a founder of communist economics and an acute and powerful
novelist.

Why Work? – Arguments for the Leisure Society

Various Writers
£6.95

"No working ideal for machine production can be based solely on the
gospel of work; still less can it be based upon an uncritical belief in
constantly raising the qualitative standard of consumption."

Visit Freedom's bookshop at 84B Whitechapel High Street,
London E1 7QX or order (postage free) from our website
at www.freedompress.org.uk